G000093678

VEGAN FOR GOOD

"If it came from a plant, eat it; if it was made in a plant, don't."
– Michael Pollan

VEGAN FOR GOOD

DELICIOUSLY SIMPLE PLANT-BASED RECIPES FOR EVERY DAY

RITA SERANO

Rita is an author, vegan food blogger, and recipe developer. She lives between the Netherlands and France with her husband and daughter, experimenting with new ideas in the quick, busy city of Amsterdam and enjoying the quiet life tending to her vegetable garden in the French countryside. Her first book, *Vegan in 7*, was also published by Kyle Books.
Instagram: @ritaserano

PHOTOGRAPHY BY CLARE WINFIELD

K

An Hachette UK Company
www.hachette.co.uk

First published in Great Britain in 2018 by
Kyle Books, an imprint of Kyle Cathie Ltd
Carmelite House
50 Victoria Embankment
London EC4Y 0DZ
www.kylebooks.co.uk

ISBN: 978 0 85783 617 5

Text copyright 2018 © Rita Serano
Design and layout copyright 2018 © Kyle Cathie
Ltd

Distributed in the US by Hachette Book Group,
1290 Avenue of the Americas, 4th and 5th Floors,
New York, NY 10104

Distributed in Canada by Canadian Manda
Group, 664 Annette St., Toronto, Ontario, Canada M6S 2C8

Rita Serano is hereby identified as the author of
this work in accordance with Section 77 of the
Copyright, Designs and Patents Act 1988.

All rights reserved. No part of this work may
be reproduced or utilised in any form or by
any means, electronic or mechanical, including
photocopying, recording or by any information
storage and retrieval system, without the prior
written permission of the publisher.

Editor: Tara O'Sullivan
Editorial Assistant: Sarah Kyle
Photographer: Clare Winfield*
Food Stylist: Joss Herd
Props Stylist: Linda Berlin
Designer: Georgia Vaux
Production: Emily Noto

* except image on page 9 – Laura Edwards

Printed and bound in China

10 9 8 7 6 5 4 3 2 1

CONTENTS

INTRODUCTION

WHY VEGAN FOR GOOD?

Well, it's simple. More and more people are choosing to eat plants and skip meat and animal products. This choice can be out of love for nature, being against animal cruelty, or love for yourself (your body). We are becoming aware of the impact animal agriculture has on our planet. We are starting to realize that if we want a livable planet, we need to change the way we eat. Animals are treated so badly in the meat industry, and it is not necessary at all. You don't need any animal products to stay healthy or alive—that is a myth. Any nutritional benefit found from eating meat can also be found from eating plants. One of the best things we can do is to eat plants. I know from my own experience that eating unprocessed, wholesome plant-based foods can give you more health, energy, and clarity. When I was in my twenties I developed an autoimmune disease, and I healed it by switching my diet to eating vegetables, fruits, grains, nuts, and seeds. I am in my forties now, and I consider myself very healthy because of my wholesome plant-based diet. I am not switching back, ever.

In my kitchen you will find nutritious, seasonal products. You might think that eating this way is difficult, lacking in flavor, expensive, and filled with unfamiliar ingredients that are hard to get. In this book I want to show you that you can eat vegan food no matter what. No matter how busy, how tired, or how uninspired you are, you can stay vegan—for good.

We all lead busy lives and time seems limited. We spend less time in the kitchen compared to the generation before us. But times are changing; people are becoming more interested in homemade food. Even if you don't always have much time to spend making it, you can still enjoy a great-tasting dinner. And if you do have time and like to cook, you can make delicious vegan meals for special occasions when friends and family come over. So there

are no excuses—you can make a fantastic dinner, lunch, or breakfast for yourself, your family, or friends using this book.

It contains four chapters: Weekends, Weekdays, No Time at All, and Sweet Celebrations. In Weekends, you will find delicious recipes for when you have more time to prepare a lovely meal for family and friends. The weekend also gives you an excellent opportunity to prepare for the week ahead, so this chapter includes some ideas and recipes to get you ready for the week.

In Weekdays, the recipes are all about getting a meal on the table within 30 minutes, plus food on the go and packed lunches. This is for when you come back from work and the kids come home from school, everyone is hungry, and you want to have dinner ready quickly.

And what about when you feel that you have genuinely No Time at All? In this chapter, I will show you how to make a delicious and nourishing meal within 15 minutes.

But staying vegan for good is not just about speed and convenience. It's also about treating family and friends and finding foods that are indulgent and delicious. So the last chapter, Sweet Celebrations, will have you whipping up all kinds of delicious treats. Even though this chapter includes cakes, puddings, and chocolate, I never use refined sugar such as white or cane sugar. Instead I choose a sweetener that is not so disruptive to your blood sugar, such as coconut sugar or maple syrup. I am always surprised to find refined sugar in all kinds of products, even in those that you wouldn't expect to contain sugar at all, like bread. (If you're interested in the consequences of eating refined sugar, I recommend watching the documentary *Fed Up* by Stephanie Soechtig.)

So there you have it—with this book I hope to give you all the tools you need to manage your time, enjoy delicious meals and treats, and ultimately stay vegan for good.

KITCHEN EQUIPMENT

Good, fast, and delicious cooking means having good tools in your kitchen. I use these daily.

A set of good-quality knives is crucial. A good sharp knife is important for cutting, slicing, and peeling. It's expensive, but it will make your cooking life so much easier. I have a large chef's knife with a blade of about 7 inches. I use it for cutting large vegetables like celery root, pumpkin, and cauliflower. I also use two types of smaller knife, both with blades of around 4 inches. One has a straight blade that is perfect for cutting smaller vegetables and fruits, or for when I have to be more precise. The other has a serrated blade, which is ideal for cutting tomatoes and delicate fruits like plums and peaches.

Next to these knives I use a **peeler** to peel vegetables and make ribbons out of carrots, cucumbers, etc. I also use a **julienne cutter** that turns vegetables into long, thin strips like spaghetti. Cutting your vegetables in different shapes will make your food more visually attractive and will give a different texture to your dishes.

Another cutting tool is a **mandoline**, a manual slicer that is ultra sharp and comes with a protector for your fingers. Take care when you use it! The mandoline is perfect for when you want to have super-thin slices that are almost transparent. If you are a bit worried about your fingers, a box grater will work instead.

A **Microplane** is a fine grater, and I use mine all the time for grating garlic, ginger, nutmeg, cinnamon, and citrus zest.

A favorite machine of mine is a **high-speed blender**. It enables me to make super-smooth sauces, creams, nut milks, banana ice cream, and soups, and it can turn oats into flour. My Vitamix has lasted me for more than a decade now, and although it was an expensive investment, it is worth the money. It is one of the most-used electrical appliances in my kitchen. But there are a lot of other great high-speed blenders from different brands, so go for the best quality you can afford.

A **food processor** with a heavy-duty motor will be very welcome in your *Vegan for Good* kitchen. They come in different sizes. Choose a size that is big enough for your needs. If you choose one with a strong motor like a Cuisinart, it will last a lifetime. If you can, get a model that comes with several attachments and different blades, including the standard metal S-blade, which you can use for chopping, crushing, grinding, and mincing, and grating and slicing discs so you can shred and slice vegetables in a jiffy. I can make homemade nut butter in this machine using whatever nuts and seeds I like.

For whipping up aquafaba (see page 135), I have a cheap **handheld mixer,** which does the job very well. If you have enough counter space, you can also use a fancier one, like a stand mixer.

Another electrical appliance that I regularly use and find very practical is a **nonstick pancake maker,** also known as a crêpe maker. I use it to make small American-style pancakes (see page 59) and my spinach-galette (see page 68). I even bake grain or bean burgers on it, too.

When discussing my kitchen utensils, I do not want to forget my cookware. I own a **heavy-bottomed cast-iron pan** that I use for cooking beans, grains, stews, and sauces. I also have a **big pot** for making soups, stocks, and pasta. My **shallow cast-iron skillet** and **good-quality nonstick ceramic pan** both come in very handy for water-frying (when cooking oil-free—see page 10). I have a **wok** for stir-fries and some **small pans** for making sauces or smaller amounts of food.

Other handy utensils include an **ice cream scoop** with a trigger. I use it for making cashew mozzarella (see page 18) and also for portioning out muffins, ice cream, cookies, burgers, falafel, etc. I also use a **mortar and pestle** for grinding spices, a **fine-mesh strainer**, a **rubber spatula**, some **wooden spoons**, a **whisk**, **wooden cutting boards**, a set of **measuring cups**, a set of measuring spoons, a pair of **kitchen scissors**, a **citrus reamer**, glass **mason jars,** and a **kitchen scale**. These kitchen tools make successful cooking so much easier.

A Note on Oven Settings

Most ovens nowadays have multiple functions, like broil, normal heat, and convection heat. Normal heat will be perfect for cooking things like cake, tarts, lasagna, and pizza. You can use the convection setting when you want a crispier effect on your food, as for vegetable fries or the crispy lentil meatballs on page 33. The temperatures in this book are for normal heat unless convection heat is specified.

INGREDIENTS

A well-stocked kitchen is essential when you want to stay *Vegan for Good*. The main ingredients I stock are fresh vegetables, fruits, and herbs, mainly organic and in season.

In my opinion, organic produce is the best choice for your own health, the health of generations to come, and the health of the planet. By choosing organic you can contribute to agricultural diversity, reduce pollution, and preserve our ecosystem. At the same time, you support (local) farming and avoid genetically engineered food. These are all big advantages, but one of the most important things is that organic food tastes great.

A lot of people will tell you that buying organic food is expensive, but if you buy in-season, local produce (for example, from a farmers' market), you can save some money. You can avoid buying the much-hyped superfoods as well, because fresh local vegetables and fruits are already superfoods–they have all the nutrients and health benefits you need.

Almost all the ingredients in this book are easy to find in food stores or big supermarkets. There may be a few you haven't heard of, like agar agar (a natural gelling agent made from seaweed), shoyu (the Japanese name for soy sauce), or aquafaba (the cooking liquid from chickpeas or white beans like cannelini). But they will soon become your friends when making delicious plant-based meals. Going to a health food store can be a fun experience, especially if you're used to shopping in a conventional supermarket. You can find new and exciting ingredients that you are not familiar with and that can change your "standard" daily meals. It changes your viewpoint and makes cooking a fun and creative process. You start to experiment. If you don't have a certain ingredient used in this book at home, feel free to swap or leave it out. You don't like cilantro? Use parsley or mint. You don't have cumin? Get another spice, like coriander seeds or a spice mix. Make a soup, stew, or salad more interesting by adding toasted seeds, nut parmesan (page 26), whole spices, or leftover bread turned into breadcrumbs. Leftovers like pesto, which is easy to keep in your fridge, lift a soup–or you can mash it with avocado and spread it on toast, or swirl it into yogurt for a nice dip. The possibilities are endless.

Cooking Without Oil

As you explore this book, you will notice that I don't often add oils (like olive or sunflower oil). I eat a diet that is as whole as possible, and I believe that oils (however natural they are) are refined products, so I try to avoid them. I choose to get my fats from avocados, nuts, seeds, and the oils that naturally occur in vegetables and grains. Instead of using oil, I cook with water, stock, or even coconut milk. I use citrus juice, balsamic vinegar, or stock to cook my oven dishes. Want some crunch on your food? Then use the oven's convection setting, which will produce crispier results. Avocado liquefied by a blender or mashed makes a great oil substitute. For dressings or sweet baking, I use 1 tablespoon mashed avocado where you would usually use 1 tablespoon oil. Another great oil substitute is fruit puree (such as banana or apple). You can use it in waffles, pancakes, or cake. Even nut butters or plant-based yogurt, in moderation, are perfect to use instead of oil. This way of cooking works for me; however, it is your choice, so feel free to add oils if you like. If you want to read more about this subject I can highly recommend books written by experts such as Dr. John McDougall (*The Starch Solution*), Dr. Caldwell Esselstyn (*Prevent and Reverse Heart Disease*), Dr. Joel Fuhrman (*Eat to Live*), and T. Colin Campbell (*The China Study*). But still, I don't want to preach, I just want to inspire people to eat more plants and show them how plants can be delicious and easy to prepare. Food must not be a religion–everyone should work out the best way of eating for themselves.

WEEKENDS

Weekends are for family and friends. You have more time to prepare a meal than during the week when, for example, the kids are at school or you are working. But on weekends you can really go for it and make a wholesome and delicious meal that takes more preparation or cooking time. I will give you my take on favorites such as a mozzarella salad and plant-based versions of some classic meat dishes such as lasagna and steak. You can even invite friends to cook with you to enjoy the process and the dinner afterward. Because I believe good food is meant to be shared!

Weekends also give you the chance to prepare food that you will be using to speed up your dishes on weekdays or when you have no time at all. So it is on the weekend that I prepare my vegetable stock, cashew sour cream, oven-roasted vegetables, and other ingredients I can use later on in the week.

VEGETABLE STOCK

If there is one ingredient that really can be a great base for lots of dishes, it must be homemade stock. For stock, I often use vegetables that aren't attractive anymore but still have lots of flavors. Choose organic products, so you can use them unpeeled, even onion skins. In this recipe I give you a few suggestions for a vegetable stock, but feel free to add more herbs, garlic, parsnips, beets, celery root, and tomatoes (you can also use nutritional yeast) when you like. The more veggies in your stock and the more time you let it simmer, the more flavorful your stock will become. Only add salt at the very last moment, or omit it to keep the stock neutral. I prefer not to use salt in my stock, as you might end up adding the stock to a dish that already contains salt. Also, salt is a very personal thing—especially if you're cooking for kids, you might choose to avoid it altogether and let people salt their own food. One final word of advice: Don't add any cruciferous vegetables (the whole cabbage family) to a vegetable stock; they will give it a bad taste, and that's a waste of your time and effort.

Makes 6½ to 7½ cups

1 leek, washed and sliced into 1-inch pieces
4 carrots, sliced into 1-inch pieces
4 celery stalks, sliced into 1-inch pieces
2 onions, quartered (leave the skins on if you use organic ones)
1 bay leaf

1 teaspoon dried thyme, or a few sprigs fresh
1 teaspoon whole black peppercorns
1 tablespoon mushroom powder (see opposite; optional)
salt or umami paste (see opposite)

Combine all the ingredients except the salt in a large pot with 2 quarts water. Put the lid on the pot and set it over high heat. Bring the water to a boil, then reduce the heat to low and simmer for 60 to 75 minutes.

Strain the stock and discard the solids. Return it to the pot and season it with salt or umami paste. Store in an airtight container in the fridge for up to 5 days or in the freezer for up to 3 months.

TIP:
I like to freeze some of the stock in ice cube trays, making it easier for portioning and perfect to use for water-frying, as I have done throughout the book.

UMAMI PASTE

Over the last few years, the biggest buzzword in cooking has been "umami." It is, in fact, the Japanese word for "yummy." But what *is* it? It is a savory taste next to sweet, salty, sour, and bitter, and it actually refers to the flavor of a glutamate that naturally occurs in meats, fish, dairy, vegetables, mushrooms, and seaweed. The taste of umami will give your dishes a hearty, meaty, and brothy flavor that leaves you feeling satisfied and comforted after eating. It is perfect for people who miss the flavors of meat when switching to a plant-based diet. This paste is for foods that could use some extra depth of flavor, such as stocks, curries, sauces, plant-based burgers, and stews. I always keep a jar in my fridge to add some extra yumminess to my dishes.

Makes about ¾ cup

2 tablespoons good-quality organic miso paste

2 tablespoons tahini or sesame paste

2 tablespoons mushroom powder (see Tip)

2 tablespoons shoyu or tamari

2 tablespoons nutritional yeast

2 tablespoons tomato concentrate

2 garlic cloves, finely chopped

Mix all the ingredients in a small bowl and store in a glass container in the fridge for up to a month.

TIP:
You can easily make mushroom powder by grinding dried mushrooms, such as porcini or shiitake, in a coffee grinder. Store the powder in an airtight container in the fridge and it will keep for at least 2 months.

CASHEW SOUR CREAM

This cultured cream is a real basic. The taste is similar to dairy-based sour cream, and it is very adaptable. For example, I use this cream as a base for dressings with other flavorings such as herbs and spices added, and as a topping for soup or porridge. I also use it to make a great mozzarella (see page 18). The fermentation part may scare you a bit, but as long as you use clean tools and hands, it always works.

Makes 2 cups

7 ounces raw cashews, soaked overnight or soaked for 1 to 2 hours in hot water

1½ tablespoons natural plant-based (coconut or soy) yogurt
½ to 1 teaspoon salt (optional)

Drain and rinse the cashews and put them in a high-speed blender. Pour in ¾ cup water and blend until the cashews are very smooth (so no lumps or grains are left). If you need to add a bit more water, start with a tablespoon at a time. However, the mixture should not be too watery. Add the yogurt and blend briefly.

Pour this mixture into a clean glass container—a mason jar is ideal. The jar should be a bit bigger than the amount of cream you have. Once you've poured in the cream, it must have some room to expand during fermentation.

Cover the jar with a piece of cheesecloth or muslin and secure it with a rubber band or some kitchen twine. Place the jar on your counter, out of direct sunlight. Let it ferment for 6 to 24 hours. As it ferments, you should see small air pockets appear. This is absolutely normal. The amount of time it needs depends on the season; on a warm day it will be ready after 6 to 10 hours, but on a colder day it needs at least 12 hours. The taste should be pleasantly tangy and refreshing.

When the cashew sour cream is done, stir in up to 1 teaspoon salt, if desired. If you're planning to use this cream to make the mozzarella on page 18, you definitely need the salt. If you want this to be a sweeter cream, leave it out. Stored in the fridge with a lid on, the cream keeps for 4 to 5 days.

Note: When you are in a hurry, you can make a simple cashew sour cream instead of the cultured version. Simply combine the drained soaked cashews, ¾ cup water, the juice of ½ lemon, and ½ to 1 teaspoon salt in a high-speed blender and blend until completely smooth. This will also keep in the fridge for 4 to 5 days.

CASHEW MOZZARELLA

Mozzarella? Yes! You can enjoy this and still be a vegan, because this version of the famous cheese is made from cashew nuts. The recipe is based on one of Myoko Schinner's from her book *The Homemade Vegan Pantry*. The mozzarella is so versatile—it is delicious in the classic Italian *caprese* salad, on a pizza, in a panini... you name it, this vegan mozzarella can do everything regular mozzarella can do.

Makes 5 large or 16 to 20 small balls

1 tablespoon agar agar
¼ cup tapioca starch
1 tablespoon nutritional yeast
1 recipe Cashew Sour Cream (see page 17; use
  either the simple or the cultured version, but be
  sure to include salt)

for the brine (optional)
2½ teaspoons good-quality salt
3¼ cups cold water

Pour ¾ cup water into a pan and set it over low heat. Add the agar agar. Cook, whisking continuously, until small bubbles form and the mixture starts to boil. Reduce the heat to its lowest setting, cover the pan, and simmer for 3 minutes.

Meanwhile, dissolve the tapioca starch in ¼ cup water and set aside. Mix the nutritional yeast into the cashew sour cream and set aside.

Uncover the pan with the agar agar mixture and add the cashew sour cream mixture while whisking thoroughly. Once mixed, add the dissolved tapioca and keep mixing until the cheese becomes all stretchy. This may take 3 to 4 minutes. Stir well, or the mixture will burn.

The mozzarella is now done. To shape it, you have two options. You can pour it into a glass mason jar, leave it to cool, then store it in the fridge. When you take it out of the jar, you can slice it. It will keep for 4 to 5 days like this.

Or, for a more traditional mozzarella look, fill a bowl with ice-cold water (or cold water with ice cubes in it) and set it nearby. Using an ice cream scoop, take a full scoop of the cheese mixture and drop it into the cold water so that a ball forms. A big scoop will give you about 5 balls, a small scoop will give you 16 to 20. Leave the mozzarella balls in the water for at least 1 hour. To store, make a brine by stirring together the salt and water in a large mason jar until the salt has dissolved. Add the mozzarella to the brine, cover, and store in the fridge for 4 to 5 days.

PEACH AND MOZZARELLA SALAD WITH BLUEBERRY BALSAMIC

This salad is great on a hot summer's day when peaches are at their best and basil is thriving in the sun. The balsamic dressing with the blueberries adds a wonderful fruity and, at the same time, sour note to the juicy sweet peaches and creamy mozzarella. A real summer delight!

Serves 2 as a lunch or 4 as a side dish

2½ ounces arugula, washed
2½ ounces baby spinach, washed
1 cucumber, cut into ribbons
3 not overly ripe peaches, pitted and cut into wedges
10½ ounces cashew mozzarella, sliced, or small whole mozzarella balls (if you haven't made mozzarella, substitute 2 avocados, sliced)
2 tablespoons chopped fresh mint or basil
½ cup almonds, chopped

for the dressing (makes 1 cup)
9 ounces blueberries (thawed, if frozen)
2¾ tablespoons good balsamic vinegar
1 tablespoon maple syrup
1 teaspoon mustard (Dijon if possible)
3 tablespoons almond butter
½ teaspoon salt, or to taste
½ teaspoon freshly ground black pepper, or to taste

Make the dressing. Combine all the dressing ingredients in a blender and blend until smooth. Taste and add more salt if needed—the flavor should be a bit tangy to contrast the sweetness of the peaches in the salad. Pour the dressing into a bowl or jar and set aside.

Arrange the arugula, spinach, cucumber ribbons, peaches, mozzarella (or avocado), and mint on a large plate and sprinkle with the chopped almonds. Serve with the dressing on the side and pour it over the salad at the last minute.

ROOT VEGETABLE FRIES WITH HOMEMADE SPICY KETCHUP

Who *doesn't* like fries? They're a real crowd-pleaser. And when made with root vegetables rather than starchy potatoes, they become altogether more interesting flavorwise. These fries are also a healthier option, as they use the oven instead of the deep fryer and are served with a batch of homemade ketchup. Now you have fries that contain less fat and a ketchup without any sugar. If you wanted to, you could eat these every day!

Serves 4

3¼ pounds root vegetables (such as sweet
  potatoes, celery root, parsnip, rutabaga,
  carrots), peeled
salt

for the ketchup
2 red onions, finely diced
2 teaspoons garlic powder
½ cinnamon stick
½ teaspoon ground allspice

1 teaspoon hot sauce (such as the sambal
  on page 90) or red pepper flakes
1½ tablespoons mushroom powder
  (see Tip, page 15)
1 teaspoon smoked paprika
2 cups tomato sauce, homemade (see Tip,
  page 30) or good-quality store-bought
3 to 4 teaspoons maple syrup
1 tablespoon white balsamic vinegar
shoyu or sea salt

Preheat the oven to 465°F (or 425°F, if using a convection oven) and line two baking sheets with parchment paper.

Bring a large pan of water to a boil. Cut the root vegetables into fries, all roughly the same shape. When the water boils, add the vegetables and blanch for 2 to 3 minutes. Drain and leave in the colander to remove as much moisture as you can. Arrange the fries in a single layer on the lined baking sheets. Sprinkle with salt to taste. Bake the fries for 25 to 30 minutes, turning them from time to time, until golden brown and crispy.

Meanwhile, make the ketchup. Water-fry the red onions in a large pan using either a little water or stock until translucent. Add the garlic powder, cinnamon, allspice, hot sauce, mushroom powder, and smoked paprika. Stir to coat the onions with the spices and cook them for a minute more. If needed, add another splash of water or stock to prevent burning. Add the tomato sauce, maple syrup, balsamic vinegar, and shoyu or salt to taste. Bring to a boil, then reduce the heat to low and simmer for 10 to 15 minutes. Let cool. (The ketchup can be made in advance. It will keep in the fridge for 10 to 14 days.)

Serve the fries with the spicy ketchup alongside.

TWO SAVORY TOPPINGS

How do you make a simple dish more interesting? Just add a bit of crunch and concentrated taste. I often make a big jar of crunchy toppings over the weekend, so when I am in a hurry later in the week making a meal such as a soup, salad, or stew, I can add a bit of these toppings to make an ordinary common dish stand out.

ALMOND AND SESAME TOPPING – Makes about 1½ cups

2 teaspoons umami paste (see page 15)
 or soy sauce
2 teaspoons maple syrup
1 teaspoon rice vinegar or balsamic vinegar
good pinch of red pepper flakes

2 teaspoons aquafaba (chickpea cooking
 liquid; see page 135)
¾ cup chopped almonds
5 tablespoons white sesame seeds
5 tablespoons black sesame seeds

Preheat the oven to 350°F and line a baking sheet with parchment paper.

Mix the umami paste, maple syrup, vinegar, red pepper flakes, and aquafaba in a small bowl. Mix the almonds and seeds in another bowl, then mix with the liquid until the nuts and seeds are fully coated.

Spread the nuts and seeds over the lined baking sheet and bake for 6 minutes in the middle of the oven, then turn the nuts and seeds and bake for 6 to 8 minutes more. Keep a close eye on them and turn again if needed—you don't want them to burn. The almonds should be golden brown and the mixture dry in the center. Remove the mixture from the oven and let cool completely, then store in a glass jar with a tight-fitting lid. It will keep at room temperature for 2 to 3 weeks.

MAPLE MUSTARD TOPPING – Makes about 2 cups

1½ teaspoons Dijon mustard

2 teaspoons maple syrup

1 teaspoon balsamic vinegar

2 teaspoons aquafaba (chickpea cooking
  liquid; see page 135)

3 tablespoons nutritional yeast

1 teaspoon dried thyme

½ teaspoon salt

½ cup rolled oats

6 tablespoons pine nuts

6 tablespoons pumpkin seeds

6 tablespoons sunflower seeds

Preheat the oven to 350°F and line a baking sheet with parchment paper. Mix the Dijon mustard, maple syrup, balsamic vinegar, aquafaba, nutritional yeast, thyme, and salt in a small bowl. In another bowl, combine the oats, pine nuts, pumpkin seeds, and sunflower seeds. Add the wet mixture to the dry mixture and stir until all the ingredients are fully coated.

Spread the mixture over the lined baking sheet and bake for 6 to 8 minutes in the middle of the oven, then turn the nuts and seeds and bake for 6 to 8 minutes more, until they are golden brown and the mixture is dry in the center. Remove the mixture from the oven and let cool completely, then store in a glass jar with a tight-fitting lid. It will keep at room temperature for 2 to 3 weeks.

NUT PARMESAN

In the past, I followed a raw diet; I did this for seven years. During this time, I learned new techniques to prepare ingredients and fun ways to swap animal-based foods for plant-based foods. One of the first (and probably one of the easiest) substitutions I learned was nut Parmesan. The secret ingredient to make it "cheesy" is nutritional yeast. This yellow yeast is flaky (like grated Parmesan) and can be found in health food stores. The nut Parmesan can (of course) be used on pasta, but it also tastes great in soups and salads, and on roasted vegetables and (plant-based) burgers. Double the recipe, if you want, because it will disappear quick!

Makes about ¾ cup

6 tablespoons pine nuts
6 tablespoons unsalted raw cashews
1 tablespoon nutritional yeast

½ teaspoon onion powder
½ teaspoon garlic powder

Combine all the ingredients in a high-speed blender and blend until broken down to the texture of grated Parmesan. Store in an airtight container in the fridge for up to a week.

> **TIP:**
> Add nuts and seeds to change the taste of this Parmesan according to your liking. Think: walnuts, blanched almonds, sunflower seeds, blanched hazelnuts, or macadamia nuts. As long as the nuts and seeds are light in color, it will be the same color as traditional Parmesan. If you like a stronger taste, you can add more nutritional yeast and salt.

FLATBREAD

From a few simple ingredients—flour, water, and salt—you can quickly make flatbreads. Known variously as tortilla, chapati, injera, roti, and matzo, flatbreads are eaten all around the world. They make a great accompaniment to or base for all kinds of dishes and are prepared quickly because they don't involve yeast. This basic recipe is simple to learn and fun to make. Don't hold back: make as many as you want and freeze them until needed.

Makes 8 large flatbreads

3½ cups whole-grain spelt flour (you can use sprouted or even a gluten-free mix)
1 teaspoon good-quality salt

2½ teaspoons baking powder
scant 1 cup hot water

Mix the flour, salt, and baking powder in a large bowl. Add the hot water and begin mixing with a fork, then switch to your hands and mix until a ball forms. Knead the dough, either in the bowl or on a clean work surface dusted with some flour, for 3 to 4 minutes, until smooth. Return the dough to the bowl, cover it with a clean, damp towel, and let rest for 15 to 30 minutes.

Divide the dough into 8 equal-size balls. On a clean, lightly floured surface, flatten one dough ball a little with your hands, then roll it out to a diameter of about 8 inches. If necessary, flour the flatbread lightly so it doesn't stick to the rolling pin or your work surface.

Place a large skillet over medium to high heat. Once the pan is hot, place a flatbread in the pan and let it cook until it starts to puff up a bit, 1 to 2 minutes. Then flip the flatbread and cook on the second side for about a minute. Transfer to a plate and cover with a clean, damp towel. Repeat until all the flatbreads are cooked.

Serve immediately or store the flatbreads in a zip-top bag in the freezer—I layer them with parchment paper between each so they can be separated easily.

BLACK BEAN QUESADILLA WITH KIWI AND JALAPEÑO SALSA VERDE

On weekdays my daughter is at school during lunch hours and I am working behind a computer screen or testing a new recipe, so lunch ends up being a quickly made sandwich, a few bites of whatever I am testing, or leftovers from the day before. On weekends we have time to sit together and eat a proper lunch with the whole family. This quesadilla is not a fast-food snack—it's a real, wholesome, home-cooked meal that can be shared with loved ones.

Serves 2 for dinner or 4 as a light lunch

for the filling
1 red onion, chopped
scant ½ cup stock or water, plus extra for frying
3 garlic cloves, finely chopped
1½ tablespoons tomato paste
1½ teaspoons dried oregano
1½ teaspoons ground cumin
1½ teaspoons chipotle powder, or 1 teaspoon smoked hot paprika
½ teaspoon ground cinnamon
½ teaspoon ground star anise
2 (15-ounce) cans black beans, drained and rinsed (or 3 cups drained cooked black beans)
½ teaspoon salt (or more to taste)

for the salsa verde
5 kiwi fruit, not overly ripe, peeled and quartered
3 scallions, finely sliced
1 jalapeño (for less heat, use ½), seeded and finely chopped, or 2 tablespoons chopped pickled jalapeño
1 bunch cilantro, washed and chopped
juice of 1 lime
½ teaspoon salt

to serve
2 flatbreads (see page 27)
2 small ripe avocados, mashed

Make the filling. Heat a nonstick skillet until hot, add the onion, and cook until lightly browned; watch carefully to be sure it doesn't burn. Add a splash of water or stock and cook, stirring and adding water or stock when needed, for 4 to 5 minutes more. Add the garlic, tomato paste, oregano, cumin, chipotle, cinnamon, and star anise. Stir to coat the onion evenly. Add the stock or water, black beans, and salt. Cook for about 8 minutes, mashing the black beans just a little so the mixture gets creamier but leaving some texture. Remove the pan from the heat.

Make the salsa by chopping all the ingredients (except the lime juice) by hand, or combine them in a food processor and pulse until finely chopped. Add the lime juice and salt, taste, and, if needed, add more.

Place one flatbread on a clean cutting board and spread all the bean mixture evenly over the bread. Now spread the mashed avocado over the bean mixture. Top with the second flatbread.

Heat a dry skillet (I like to use a cast-iron one) and toast the quesadilla on each side for a few minutes. To flip the quesadilla more easily, invert the pan over a large plate and then slide the quesadilla back into the pan. Cut the quesadilla into 6 to 8 pieces and spoon over the kiwi salsa.

SLOW-ROASTED CHERRY TOMATOES

In late summer, when tomatoes are at their very best, I always end up buying way too many so, to preserve them, I slow-roast tomatoes in the oven. Slow-roasting intensifies the flavors. For a real flavor hit, add some to salads, bowls, lunches or pasta. Otherwise, blend them into an incredibly flavored tomato sauce, which can also be used in other dishes, like homemade ketchup (see page 22) or simply spread the sauce on a flatbread to make a super-quick pizza (see page 62).

Makes 1 to 1½ pounds

2¼ pounds cherry tomatoes, halved
2 tablespoons white balsamic vinegar
1 to 2 garlic cloves, chopped

¾ teaspoon good-quality coarse sea salt
 (preferably smoked)
a few sprigs of thyme (optional)

Preheat the oven to 265°F. Mix the cherry tomatoes, balsamic vinegar, garlic, salt, and thyme in a bowl. Spread the mixture over a rimmed baking sheet and bake for 3 to 4 hours.

When the tomatoes are ready, they will be soft and have released their juices. Remove from the oven and let cool completely. Store in an airtight container in the fridge for 4 to 5 days.

TIP:
Blend the tomatoes to make 2 cups of incredibly delicious tomato sauce that can be used in pasta dishes, stews, and curries or as a base for a pizza.

PERFECTLY COOKED LENTILS

Lentils—whether Puy, beluga, or plain brown—are one of my favorite ingredients. They don't require pre-soaking, unlike larger legumes. They keep their shape really well, and they can be added to lots of dishes and transformed into entirely new recipes. I usually make a large batch over the weekend so I can grab them easily out of the fridge as I need them throughout the week. Cooking lentils yourself saves you money (buying individual cans or jars is much more expensive), avoids extra packaging (meaning less waste), and ensures they are (of course) very delicious. The key to cooking lentils is thorough rinsing. Boil them with aromatics to get even more taste. One note: Do not add any salt while boiling, because salt slows down the whole cooking process, which results in tougher skins. Add salt *after* the lentils have been cooked.

Makes 6 to 7 cups

1 pound dried Puy, beluga, or brown lentils
1 head garlic, sliced in half horizontally
1 onion, halved
1 teaspoon fennel seeds

1 bay leaf, cracked
1 teaspoon dried thyme (optional)
1 teaspoon red pepper flakes (optional)
salt

Rinse the lentils thoroughly in a colander under cold running water. Transfer them to a large pot and add 6 cups cold water, the garlic, onion, fennel seeds, bay leaf, and the thyme and chile (if using).

Bring to a boil over medium-high heat, skimming off and discarding any foam that appears on the surface (this can contain impurities that you did not catch with the rinsing).

Once the water boils, reduce the heat to low and simmer for 20 minutes, until the lentils are cooked but still a bit firm when you bite into

them—"al dente," as the Italians say. If you prefer them softer, add 3 to 5 minutes to the cooking time, but no longer, or the lentils will start to fall apart.

Turn off the heat and add salt to taste. Let cool completely, then transfer to an airtight container and store in the fridge or freezer. If you decide to freeze the lentils, I'd suggest freezing them in four batches of 1 to 1½ cups each, as these are more suitable amounts for smaller households and will be easier to defrost.

TIP:
For extra depth of flavor, mix 1 or 2 tablespoons umami paste (see page 15) with 1 tablespoon water and add to the cooked lentils instead of salt.

LENTIL AND MUSHROOM "MEATBALLS" WITH TOMATO SAUCE

One might think of meatballs in tomato sauce as a typical traditional Italian dish, but it is actually more American Italian. In the early twentieth century, meat was expensive, and many families in Italy were poor. They were used to eating pasta and tomato sauce with only a bit of meat or none at all. Around this time, many Italians emigrated to America in search of a better life. In time, as their standards of living improved, the "bits of meat" became "meatballs." This shows how dishes can be transformed over time. I wanted to transform this dish even further, so I have changed the "meatballs" into mushroom and lentil balls.

Serves 4 (makes about 20 "meatballs")

1 medium onion, chopped
9 ounces button mushrooms (or other variety), chopped
¼ cup stock or water, plus extra for frying
2 garlic cloves, chopped
2 teaspoons dried oregano
½ teaspoon ground fennel seeds (you can easily grind the seeds using a mortar and pestle)
½ teaspoon ground chile
1 heaping teaspoon tomato paste
8½ ounces drained cooked green or beluga lentils (see opposite, or from a 14-ounce jar or can), roughly mashed with a fork
1¼ cups cooked bulgur wheat (or quinoa or rice)
½ cup rolled oats
4 teaspoons nutritional yeast (optional)
2 cups homemade tomato sauce (see page 30)
small bunch of basil (optional), leaves torn
salt and freshly ground black pepper
10½ ounces whole-grain pasta of choice, to serve

Preheat the oven to 425°F (or 400°F, if using a convection oven) and line a baking sheet with parchment paper.

Heat a nonstick skillet until hot and add the onions and mushrooms with a splash of stock or water. Allow them to start to caramelize and, if needed, add some extra stock or water (a splash at a time). Once the onions and mushrooms have softened, add the garlic, herbs, spices and tomato paste. Add the ¼ cup stock and cook for 4 to 5 minutes.

Remove the pan from the heat and tip the mixture into a large bowl. Add the lentils, cooked bulgur, rolled oats, and nutritional yeast. Mix thoroughly and add salt and pepper to taste. (You can also mix this in a food processor by pulsing a couple of times to combine.)

Make small balls of this mixture, either using a small ice cream scoop or by rolling about 1½ tablespoonful into a ball with clean, moist hands. Set each ball on the lined baking sheet and continue until all the mixture is gone. Bake for 20 minutes—you want them a little crisp on the outside and moist inside.

Meanwhile warm the tomato sauce and add most of the torn basil leaves, reserving some of

continued

⟶ the basil for later. Let the sauce simmer while the "meatballs" bake.

Cook the pasta according to the package instructions. Once cooked, drain the pasta in a colander, reserving some of the cooking liquid.

Return the pasta to the pan and add a couple of tablespoons of the cooking liquid. (This prevents the pasta from sticking together without you having to add any oil.) Add the balls to the sauce. Serve the pasta topped with the balls and sauce and garnished with the reserved fresh basil.

TIP:
These "faux" meatballs have an Italian seasoning, but they can easily be adapted to other flavors as well. Use 1 teaspoon ground cumin, 1 teaspoon oregano, and 1 teaspoon paprika and serve it with the kiwi salsa from page 28 for a Mexican-inspired dish. Add 1 to 2 tablespoons of your favorite curry paste and serve the meatballs with cooked or stir-fried noodles to make the dish more Asian-themed. For a North African taste, add 1 teaspoon ground cumin, 1 teaspoon ground coriander, ½ teaspoon ground cinnamon, and 1 to 2 teaspoons harissa paste.

WHOLE ROASTED CELERY ROOT

I like to roast my vegetables whole. The skin acts as a natural alternative to foil and retains all the moisture. This way of cooking is fuss-free, has no waste (e.g., aluminium foil), and really makes the flavor of the vegetable stand out. Use the roasted celery root in soups, stews, salad, or as a celery root "steak" (see page 38).

Makes 8 slices

1 whole celery root, well washed (or scrubbed, if needed)

Preheat the oven to 400°F. Place the whole celery root in a baking dish and roast for 1½ to 2 hours, until you can easily pierce it through with a knife. Remove the celery root from the oven and let cool.

When the celery root is cool enough to handle, cut off the skin using a sharp knife, then cut it horizontally into 8 slices about ¾ inch thick. Store the slices in an airtight container in the fridge to use later in the week, or serve them right away as celery root "steaks" (see page 38).

GRILLED CELERY ROOT "STEAKS" WITH CASHEW TARTAR SAUCE

It's easy to make "steaks" from slices of whole roasted celery root. You can cook them on a grill pan, or in the summer, put them on your outdoor grill.

Serves 4

8 cooked celery root slices (see page 37)

for the tartar sauce
2 cups Cashew Sour Cream (see page 17)
6 tablespoons chopped sour gherkins
  (ensure they are sugar-free)
6 tablespoons chopped capers

½ cup fresh flat-leaf parsley, chopped
1 tablespoon Dijon mustard
juice of ½ lemon
salt and freshly ground black pepper

green salad and cooked grains or potatoes,
  to serve

Heat a cast-iron grill pan over high heat or preheat a panini press according to the manufacturer's instructions. Once hot, add as many celery root slices as will fit in the pan, leaving enough room to flip them (you may have to do this in batches). Cook the steaks on one side for 2 to 3 minutes, until grill marks form. Flip them over and cook for 2 to 3 minutes on the second side. Transfer the steaks to a plate, set another plate on top, and keep warm in a low oven while you cook the remaining steaks and get the sauce ready.

Make the tartar sauce. Mix all the tartar sauce ingredients in a medium bowl and add salt and pepper to taste.

Serve the steaks with the sauce on the side, along with a green salad and some cooked grains or potatoes.

SAVORY BEET MUFFINS

Cake salé ("salty" or savory cake) is not part of Dutch cuisine. But after I was introduced to it by a French friend, I really wanted to make my own savory cake. The key feature of the cake is that it's light in texture. Normal cakes and muffins use eggs to accomplish this, but here aquafaba gives these hearty muffins a nice airy touch. Beets are naturally a bit sweet, so these savory muffins benefit from the contrast provided by the salty olives. All in all, I think I've succeeded in my mission to make a vegan *cake salé*.

Makes 10 to 12 muffins

½ cup pumpkin seeds
1½ raw medium red beets, peeled
6 tablespoons aquafaba (chickpea cooking liquid; see page 135), chilled
1½ cups whole-grain spelt flour
50g oat flakes
2 teaspoons baking powder
1 teaspoon baking soda

2 tablespoons nutritional yeast (optional)
1 teaspoon salt
1 teaspoon freshly ground black pepper
1¼ cups natural plant-based yogurt
1 small bunch chives, finely chopped
2 tablespoons chopped fresh thyme
2½ ounces pitted black olives, chopped

Preheat the oven to 400°F. Line a muffin tin with paper liners.

Toast the pumpkin seeds in a cast-iron or nonstick pan until they start to pop. Transfer to a plate and set aside.

Finely grate the beet using a food processor, mandoline, or box grater. Set aside.

Whip the aquafaba in a clean bowl using a handheld mixer or in the bowl of a stand mixer fitted with the whisk attachment until stiff white peaks form.

In another bowl, mix the flour, oat flakes, baking powder, baking soda, nutritional yeast (if using), salt, and pepper.

In a blender, combine the yogurt and beet and blend until well combined. Add this to the flour mixture, then add the herbs, olives, and whipped aquafaba. Mix gently until all the ingredients have been combined.

Divide the mixture evenly among the wells of the prepared muffin tin. (You can use an ice cream scoop to make the muffins the same size.) Scatter over the pumpkin seeds. Bake for 20 to 25 minutes, until a wooden skewer inserted into a muffin comes out clean. Remove from the oven and leave them to cool.

Once the muffins are baked, you'll notice that the vibrant pink color has faded—this is normal.

TIP:
You can take the muffins with you for a quick lunch or serve them with a salad and some Cashew Sour Cream (see page 17).

PICKLES

The process of making pickles is one of the oldest methods of food preserving. There are two ways of pickling: with vinegar or with salt. The term *pickling* actually comes from the Dutch word *pekel* ("brine" in English), which means "salt." By preserving food this way, Dutch navigators could easily take supplies with them on their ships. But pickling is not typically Dutch; think of German sauerkraut, Korean kimchi, Japanese *tsukemono*, and olives. Pickles make a delicious side dish to heavier and fatty dishes. Flavorwise, I think they make a meal far more interesting.

PICKLED RED ONIONS – Makes 1 pint

4 medium red onions
½ teaspoon coriander seeds
½ teaspoon whole black peppercorns

½ teaspoon salt
¾ cup raw apple cider vinegar

Peel the onions and thinly slice into half-moons (you can use a mandoline). Place in a 1-pint glass jar with a tight-fitting lid, packing them in tightly. Add the spices and salt. Pour in the vinegar and add enough water to submerge the onions. Seal the jar and set aside at room temperature for at least 3 to 4 hours or, better still, overnight. The pickles will keep in the fridge for up to a month.

SPICY PICKLED CARROTS – Makes two 1-pint jars

1 pound (rainbow) carrots
1 teaspoon cumin seeds
2 garlic cloves, roughly chopped
1 (¾-inch) piece fresh ginger, peeled and
  roughly chopped

1 red chile, seeded and sliced
1 cup water
1 cup raw apple cider vinegar
¾ teaspoon salt

Scrub the carrots and cut them into any shape you desire; I like to either julienne them or cut them into thin rounds. Toast the cumin seeds in a dry pan over low heat for a minute or so, until they are fragrant. Divide the seeds between two 1-pint glass jars with tight-fitting lids. Divide the garlic, ginger, and chile between the jars, then add the carrots. Combine the water, vinegar, and salt in a large pan and bring the mixture to a gentle boil. Stir until the salt has dissolved, then pour the pickling liquid over the carrots in the jars, leaving about a ½-inch gap at the top (you may not have to use all the pickling liquid). Seal the jars and shake them to remove any air pockets. Let cool completely, then refrigerate for 2 to 3 days to develop flavor before eating. The pickles will keep in the fridge for at least a month.

LASAGNA WITH LENTIL RAGÙ AND CAULIFLOWER BÉCHAMEL

Lasagna is a crowd-pleasing dish with its comforting flavors. It's perfect for when guests are coming—you can prepare the lasagna ahead of time and pop it in the oven when they arrive. I swapped the traditional meat-based sauce for a lentil-and-tomato ragù and the milk-based béchamel for a creamy cashew sauce.

Serves 6

9 ounces dried lasagna noodles of your choice (spelt, whole-grain, gluten-free, etc.)

for the lentil ragù
2 carrots, grated
1 onion, finely diced
9 ounces mushrooms, roughly chopped
1 zucchini, grated
5 garlic cloves, chopped
½ teaspoon ground chile (or more to taste)
3 cups tomato puree
1 tablespoon mushroom powder (see Tip, page 15)
1 tablespoon maple syrup (optional)
1 pound drained cooked lentils (see page 32, or from two 14-ounce cans)
2 teaspoons dried oregano
1 bunch of basil, roughly chopped
1¼ cups vegetable stock (see page 14) or water, plus more for cooking
salt

for the béchamel
14 ounces cauliflower florets
1¾ cups cashews, soaked and drained
¾ cup vegetable stock (see page 14) or hot water
3 tablespoons nutritional yeast
¼ to ½ teaspoon freshly grated nutmeg
salt

Preheat the oven to 350°F.

Make the ragù. Heat a large nonstick skillet and add the carrots, onion, mushrooms, and zucchini. Water-fry them with 2 tablespoons of stock or water until the vegetables are soft and translucent, 8 to 10 minutes. Then stir in the garlic and chile and cook for 2 minutes more. Add the tomato puree, mushroom powder, maple syrup, lentils, oregano, basil, stock, and salt to taste. Bring to a boil, then reduce the heat to low and simmer for 15 to 20 minutes.

Meanwhile, make the béchamel. Bring a pan of water to a boil, add the cauliflower florets, and cook until they are soft and you can easily pierce one with a sharp knife. Drain the florets and transfer them to a blender. Add the cashews, stock, nutritional yeast, salt, and nutmeg. Blend until completely smooth. Set aside.

When the ragù is ready, assemble the lasagna. Spread a little ragù over the bottom of a large (mine is 8 x 12 inches), high-sided baking dish. Top with a layer of lasagna noodles, then a layer of ragù. Continue to layer the lasagna noodles and ragù until the baking dish is almost full and you have used up all the ragù. Top the lasagna with the béchamel and transfer the dish to the middle rack of your oven. Bake for 45 minutes, then remove from the oven. Let it cool for 10 minutes before serving.

PEANUT AND SWEET POTATO SOUP

Peanut soup is a popular dish in Indonesian and Surinam restaurants in the Netherlands, but it originates from Africa and is very well known in countries like Ghana, Nigeria and Gambia. Usually it is a soup or a stew made of ground peanuts, tomatoes, other vegetables and often chicken, served with rice, millet or sweet potatoes. My version is made with peanut butter and, instead of serving the soup with sweet potatoes, I use them in the soup itself. Make sure you use a good-quality peanut butter that only contains peanuts and salt. Avoid ones using palm oil and sugar.

Serves 4 as a main, 6 to 8 as a starter or lunch

1 teaspoon cumin seeds
1 teaspoon coriander seeds
1 onion, diced
4 or 5 garlic cloves
½ teaspoon ground cinnamon
½ teaspoon ground allspice
1 red chile, seeded and chopped
2 to 3 tomatoes, chopped
1¼ to 1½ pounds sweet potato, peeled and cut
  into ¾-inch cubes
scant ½ cup peanut butter
4 cups vegetable stock (see page 14) or water

3½ ounces kale or cavolo nero, torn
1½ cups drained cooked black lentils or black
  beans (or one 15-ounce can, drained
  and rinsed)
salt

for the topping
6 tablespoons Cashew Sour Cream (see page 17)
  or coconut yogurt
fresh cilantro, chopped
fresh chile, chopped

Toast the cumin and coriander seeds in a large dry skillet until fragrant. Add the onions and a splash of stock or water. Sauté until the onions are translucent, 4 to 5 minutes. If needed, add a bit more stock or water. Add the garlic, cinnamon, allspice, chile, tomatoes, and sweet potato and stir until all the ingredients are coated with the spices. Cook for 2 minutes more, then, working quickly, add the peanut butter and stir until it has dissolved—you need to work fast or the peanut butter will stick to the pan.

Pour in the stock and bring to a boil. Reduce the heat to medium and simmer for 18 to 20 minutes, until the sweet potato is soft and cooked through. Puree the soup in a blender or with an immersion blender until smooth. Return the soup to the pan and add the kale and beans. Cook for 2 to 4 minutes more, until the kale has wilted and the beans are warm. Add salt to taste. Serve in bowls, topped with a swirl of cashew sour cream and fresh cilantro and chile. The soup also freezes well.

TIP:
Sprinkle Almond and Sesame Topping (see page 24) over the soup for extra flavor. You can add cooked grains like rice or quinoa to the soup as well.

CRUNCHY SALAD WITH AVOCADO HERBED DRESSING

This salad isn't new; in fact, it is based on two famous recipes: Waldorf salad and Green Goddess dressing. The first was created in the Waldorf Astoria hotel in New York back in 1896 and originally had celery, walnuts, apples, and grapes dressed with mayonnaise. The Green Goddess dressing was created in the Palace Hotel in San Francisco in 1923, and its original ingredients were scallions, parsley, tarragon, anchovies and mayonnaise. Of course, here I omit the anchovies and make an egg-free mayonnaise.

Serves 4

for the salad
5 celery stalks, thinly sliced
2 fennel bulbs, thinly sliced
2 green apples, quartered, cored, and thinly sliced
5¼ ounces salad leaves, such as watercress

for the dressing
1 ripe avocado, halved and pitted
scant ½ cup natural plant-based yogurt
1 or 2 garlic cloves
3 tablespoons raw apple cider vinegar
3 tablespoons mixed chopped fresh parsley, chives, and dill
½ teaspoon salt or white miso paste
freshly ground black pepper

Make the dressing. Combine all the dressing ingredients in a blender and blend until smooth. Check the seasoning, then pour into a bowl.

Combine the salad ingredients in a large bowl or on a serving plate. Serve the salad with the dressing on top.

TIP:
You can use the Maple Mustard Topping (see page 25) for some extra crunch.

WHOLE ROASTED CAULIFLOWER, SPICED RICE, AND FRESH GREEN CHUTNEY

Cauliflower rice, cauliflower steak, cauliflower wings, cauliflower puree, cauliflower pasta sauce . . . who knew this humble vegetable was going to be such a hip ingredient? And for a good reason—you can do a lot with cauliflower, because it tastes quite mild and adapts easily to any flavorings you add to it. I really like to serve a whole roasted cauliflower as a centerpiece when having guests.

Serves 4

1 whole head cauliflower, outer leaves removed
1 teaspoon cumin seeds
1 teaspoon coriander seeds
½ teaspoon fennel seeds
1 teaspoon mustard seeds (optional)
1 teaspoon garam masala
1 teaspoon your favorite curry powder
1 teaspoon ground chile
1 tablespoon chopped fresh ginger
1 onion, finely chopped
3 tablespoons vegetable stock or water
1 (14-ounce) can peeled tomatoes, chopped
3 tablespoons chopped fresh cilantro, to serve
salt

for the rice

1 cinnamon stick
½ teaspoon whole cloves
8 whole cardamom pods
1⅔ cups brown basmati rice, washed
1 bay leaf
2½ cups vegetable stock or water

for the chutney

1 bunch of cilantro, chopped
1 bunch of mint, chopped
juice of ½ lemon or lime
½ teaspoon cumin seeds
1 green chile, seeded (leave them
  in if you like it hot)
1 garlic clove, chopped
2 scallions, chopped
3 tablespoons coconut yogurt
½ teaspoon salt

Preheat the oven to 350°F.

Remove the stem and part of the core of the cauliflower—be careful not to remove too much, as the core holds the head of cauliflower together.

Toast the cumin, coriander, fennel, and mustard seeds (if using) in a dry pan over low heat until fragrant. Add the garam masala, curry powder, fresh ginger, onion, and 3 tablespoons water or stock. Stir-fry over medium heat until the onion is soft and translucent. Add the tomatoes and bring to a boil. Reduce the heat to low and simmer for 10 minutes.

Place the cauliflower cored-side down in a deep baking dish or cast-iron skillet and pour over the sauce. Put the lid on the pan or cover the cauliflower with a sheet of foil. Bake for 1 hour, then uncover and bake for 30 minutes more, or until the cauliflower is cooked through and can

continued ⟶

⟶ be easily pierced with a sharp knife. Meanwhile, make the rice. Toast the cinnamon, cloves, and cardamom in a small dry pan over medium heat until fragrant.

In a large pan, combine the rice, bay leaf, toasted spices, and stock or water. Cook the rice according to the instructions on the package. Once cooked, remove from the heat and set aside with the lid on.

Make the chutney. Combine all the chutney ingredients in a food processor (reserve some of the cilantro for garnish) and pulse until the mixture is quite smooth, almost like a pesto. Set aside.

Transfer the roasted cauliflower to a serving plate and scatter the reserved cilantro over the top. Serve the cauliflower with the rice and chutney alongside.

TIP:
Because the roasted cauliflower itself is quite subtle in flavor, you can transform it to any taste you like. Rub the cauliflower with a mixture of 2 to 3 tablespoons tomato paste, harissa to taste, and a squeeze of lemon juice for a more North African feel. Use 2 tablespoons curry paste, 1 teaspoon fresh lime juice, and some coconut milk for an Asian-inspired cauliflower. Thin the umami paste from page 15 with some water or rice vinegar (so it resembles mayonnaise) for a Japanese-style cauliflower, or make a South American version with the chimichurri from page 76.

ROAST PUMPKIN

My favorite way of preparing pumpkin or squash is to roast them in the oven. Because I don't use a lot of oil in my cooking (see page 10), when roasting pumpkin I substitute balsamic vinegar, orange juice, stock, or water. I often make a big batch of roast pumpkin for the whole week so that I can make a quick and healthy meal on days when I have less time. I use the roasted pumpkin in salads, soups, grain bowls, and pasta dishes, and for packed lunches.

Serves 4 as a main

1 (2¼- to 3¼-pound) pumpkin or winter squash, such as butternut, red kuri, or kabocha
2 red onions, peeled
1 teaspoon red pepper flakes

1 teaspoon sea salt
2 to 3 tablespoons white balsamic vinegar, vegetable stock, or water

---

Preheat the oven to 400°F and line a baking sheet with parchment paper.

Halve and then quarter the pumpkin and remove the seeds with a spoon. Peel off the skin with a small knife or vegetable peeler. Now cut the pumpkin into ¾- to 1-inch cubes. Cut the onions into ½- to ¾-inch dice. Transfer the pumpkin and onions to a large bowl and add the red pepper flakes, salt, and vinegar. Mix the vegetables until they are all coated with the spices, salt, and vinegar. Spread the mixture over the lined baking sheet, leaving enough space between the cubes for them to cook evenly. Bake for 25 to 30 minutes in the middle of the oven, turning halfway through the cooking time, until the pumpkin is soft but still hold its shape. Use immediately or let cool completely and store in an airtight container in the fridge.

GRILLED RADICCHIO, BAKED PUMPKIN, BEAN PUREE, AND GREMOLATA

Gremolata is a mixture of lemon zest, garlic, and parsley. Italians will know it for its use in the meat dish osso buco, but I think it goes very well with vegetables, too: for example, in this autumn recipe of radicchio, pumpkin, and beans.

Serves 4

1¾ cups vegetable stock (see page 14)
2 (15-ounce) cans white beans, drained
    and rinsed (or 3 cups drained cooked
    white beans)
1 head radicchio, sliced into 8 wedges
1 to 2 tablespoons balsamic vinegar
½ recipe Roast Pumpkin (see page 53;
  cut the pumpkin into wedges instead of cubes)
salt and freshly ground black pepper

for the gremolata
1 teaspoon lemon zest
small bunch of parsley, chopped
1 garlic clove, finely grated
Maple and Mustard Topping (see page 25),
  to serve

Preheat the broiler and line a baking sheet with parchment paper.

Put the stock in a medium pan and bring to a boil. Add the beans and simmer for 5 to 7 minutes. Drain the beans, reserving the stock, and transfer them to a blender with about 6 tablespoons of the reserved stock. Blend until smooth, adding a bit more of the reserved stock if necessary, but be careful not to add too much liquid—you want the beans to have the same consistency as mashed potatoes. (You can also mash the beans with a potato masher; this will give them a more rustic look.) Taste and add salt and pepper if needed. Return the beans to the pan and keep them warm over very low heat, stirring from time to time to prevent burning.

While the beans are cooking, lay the radicchio wedges on the lined baking sheet. Sprinkle over the balsamic vinegar and season with salt and pepper. Broil the wedges for 5 to 6 minutes, turning them regularly so that they don't burn.

Make the gremolata. Mix the lemon zest, parsley, and garlic with a good pinch of salt in a bowl.

When the radicchio wedges are cooked, you can start plating. Begin by adding a bit of bean puree to the individual plates, top with the broiled radicchio and pumpkin wedges, then sprinkle over some of the gremolata and the maple and mustard topping. Ready to serve!

TIP:
This is great served with the balsamic reduction on page 86.

SPRING VEGETABLE PACKETS

En *papillotte* is the French term for baking food enclosed in a parchment paper packet so the food steams gently in the hot oven. This method of preparing food is also healthy and clean—you don't have to add any oil. I let my guests open the packets at the table so they can enjoy the release of aromas and flavors of the vegetables.

Serves 4

2 lemons, each cut into 8 slices

1 bunch radishes, greens removed, halved

1 bunch asparagus, woody ends trimmed, cut into 1-inch pieces

1 head broccoli, cut into small florets

7 ounces fava beans (thawed, if frozen)

1 small garlic clove, finely chopped (optional)

1 teaspoon red pepper flakes (optional)

4 tablespoons water or vegetable stock (see page 14)

to serve

Cashew Sour Cream (see page 17)

small bunch of fresh soft herbs—parsley, tarragon, dill, or chives (or a mix of these), finely chopped

---

Preheat the oven to 400°F. Cut four 12-inch squares of parchment paper and lay them open on your work surface. Place 2 slices of lemon on each sheet. In a large bowl, combine the radishes, asparagus, broccoli, and fava beans and add salt, garlic, and red pepper flakes (if using) to taste. Distribute the vegetables evenly among the four sheets. Working with one sheet at a time, bring the edges of the paper together to form a packet and spoon in 1 tablespoon of stock or water. Bind the packet at the top with kitchen twine so it is completely sealed.

Repeat to make three additional packets.

Place the packets on a baking sheet and bake for 25 minutes. Open one packet to see if your vegetables are cooked; they still should have a little bite. If they are not cooked, close the packet again and bake for 5 minutes more.

Serve with a dollop of cashew sour cream and some chopped fresh herbs scattered over the top.

TIP:

I like to serve the packets with new potatoes or polenta.

WHOLE-GRAIN PANCAKES WITH CHERRY COMPOTE

Pancakes, or *Pannenkoeken*, as we call them, have a special place in Dutch food culture. Having pancakes at a party or for dinner is seen as a real treat. Ask a Dutch child what would be good to eat for dinner, and the answer will be pancakes with apple syrup or sugar. My girl doesn't agree at all with the traditional Dutch pancakes; in fact, I always have to make something different for her if pancakes are eaten on special occasions. The ones she really likes are small, American-style pancakes, which I sometimes serve for breakfast. This recipe makes quite a few pancakes, because I like to freeze them so during the week, I can grab some from the freezer and reheat them in the oven.

Makes 20 to 22 (4-inch) pancakes

for the pancakes
2⅓ cups whole-grain spelt flour (or use gluten-free flour, if you prefer)
3 cups plant-based milk
1½ teaspoons baking powder
pinch of salt
2 tablespoons chia seeds
3 tablespoons maple syrup

for the cherry compote
1 pound pitted cherries (thawed, if frozen)
juice of 2 oranges
½ teaspoon vanilla powder
1 teaspoon ground ginger
2 teaspoons ground cinnamon
2 teaspoons arrowroot powder or cornstarch
handful of raw almonds, chopped, to serve

Make the pancake batter. Combine all the pancake ingredients in a large bowl. Whisk until no lumps remain and set aside for 10 minutes (you can also do this the night before and keep the batter in the fridge, covered, until ready to cook the pancakes).

Heat a nonstick skillet. Pour in 2 tablespoons of batter per pancake. Depending on the size of your pan, you may be able to cook several at once. Cook until small holes appear and the surface of the pancakes is dry, then flip them and cook for 1 to 2 minutes on the second side. Keep the cooked pancakes warm between two plates in the oven on the lowest temperature while you cook the remaining batter.

While the pancakes cook, make the cherry compote. Put the cherries, orange juice, vanilla, ginger, and cinnamon in a small pan over medium-low heat. When the compote starts to simmer, reduce the heat to low and simmer for a further 5 minutes. Combine the arrowroot and 2 tablespoons of water in a small bowl. Add this mixture to the cherry compote and stir well. Cook for 1 minute more, or until the compote thickens.

Serve the pancakes topped with the cherry compote and some chopped almonds.

TIP:
If you would like to freeze any of your pancakes, stack them with parchment paper between them so that it is easier to separate them.

WEEKDAYS

During the workweek, you have less time to spend on cooking, but you still want something delicious and healthy, an, if you have a family, you will want to give your kids the best you can. Nowadays a lot of people opt for prepared meals from the supermarket because they are fast and easy, and there is no cooking involved. But these meals are full of fats and refined sugars, not many are vegan, and they are expensive. In this chapter I will show you vegan dishes that don't take longer than 30 minutes to prepare. These are dishes you can take with you or that can be eaten the next day. With some planning and preparation over the weekend, you can eat vegan during the week as well. It is not complicated at all!

SPRING GREEN CHICKPEA PIZZA

I don't always have the time or the patience to make a yeast-based pizza dough. You have to knead it, stretch it, shape it, and let rest. All that takes time. So in this recipe, I use a chickpea crust. Now you only need to mix chickpea flour with some water and salt to make a dough. The name of this recipe sums up both the color and the components of this wonderful pizza. It takes minimal effort for maximum result!

Serves 4 for a light lunch or 2 as a main

for the pizza crust
2¾ cups chickpea flour, sifted
1 teaspoon salt
freshly ground black pepper

for the pesto sauce
1 large bunch basil, chopped
  (reserve some whole leaves for garnish)
½ avocado, pitted and peeled

5 tablespoons pine nuts
juice of ½ lemon
1 garlic clove, finely chopped
2 tablespoons nutritional yeast (optional)

toppings
1 zucchini, shaved lengthwise into ribbons
½ bunch asparagus, shaved into ribbons
3 scallions, sliced into ¼-inch-wide pieces
2½ ounces pitted green olives (optional)
2 tablespoons pine nuts

Preheat the oven to its highest setting. In a large bowl, whisk together the chickpea flour, 2 cups water, the salt, and some pepper until no lumps remain. If you have 5 minutes to spare, set the batter aside—this will improve the batter. Pour the mixture into a nonstick rimmed baking sheet (about 8 x 12 inches). (If the baking sheet isn't nonstick, line it with parchment paper.) Bake for 13 to 15 minutes, until the pizza crust has set.

Meanwhile, make the pesto. Combine all the pesto ingredients in a food processor and process until smooth. If needed, add a splash of water to keep the machine going. Taste and adjust the seasoning if needed, then pour the pesto into a bowl and set aside.

When the pizza crust is cooked, remove it from the oven and switch on the broiler. Spread the pesto over the crust and scatter the toppings evenly over the pesto. Broil for 3 to 5 minutes, keeping an eye on the pizza to ensure the toppings do not burn. Serve garnished with the reserved basil leaves.

PIPERADE

I love watching cooking shows, especially those on the BBC channels. I remember once watching an episode of Keith Floyd where he made piperade, a Basque dish of cooked onions, peppers, and tomatoes, in the kitchen of a Frenchwoman. She wasn't impressed by his cooking and she told him clearly how she felt a real piperade should be made. She liked only the traditional version of this famous dish—not Keith's—and I don't think she would approve of my version, either. Nonetheless, it's a perfectly delicious vegan variation of the classic.

Serves 2

1 (9-ounce) block medium-firm tofu,
  drained
2 red onions, diced
1 red bell pepper, sliced
1 yellow bell pepper, sliced
4 garlic cloves, finely chopped
4 medium tomatoes, chopped

pinch of ground turmeric (optional)
1 small bunch flat-leaf parsley, chopped
kala namak (Indian black salt), if available,
  or another good-quality salt
freshly ground black pepper
toasted bread, cooked grains, or potatoes,
  to serve

Crumble the tofu with a fork in a bowl (it should end up looking like scrambled egg) and set aside.

Heat a nonstick or cast-iron pan over high heat. Add the onions and a touch of water (or stock, if you have some). Cook until the onions are soft and golden, 5 to 7 minutes, adding a little more liquid if needed. Reduce the heat to medium and add the bell peppers, garlic, and tomatoes.

Stir to combine, then cook for 6 to 8 minutes to soften the peppers and tomatoes. Add the crumbled tofu, along with the turmeric (if using). Season with kala namak and black pepper to taste. Cook for 1 to 2 minutes more, until the tofu is warmed through. Sprinkle with parsley and serve with toasted bread, cooked grains, or potatoes for a more filling meal.

VEGAN "EGG" SALADS

In the late seventies and eighties, egg salads were the fashionable thing to make when you threw a party. I remember watching my grandma making egg salad every time we had a family get-together. In memory of those happy family occasions, I really wanted to create a vegan version of an egg salad. These salads are super easy to make and are great on toast, in a wrap, served with grains and greens, etc. The trick is to use kala namak, or Indian black salt, because it gives the dish its "eggy" taste.

CHICKPEA CURRIED "EGG" SALAD – Makes enough filling for 2 wraps

1 (14½-ounce) can chickpeas, drained and rinsed or 1½ cups drained cooked chickpeas

1 generous teaspoon of your favorite curry powder

½ teaspoon kala namak (Indian black salt) or another good-quality salt

5 tablespoons natural plant-based yogurt

Roughly mash the beans with a fork in a bowl. Do not mash them completely; you want to keep some texture. Add the curry powder, kala namak, and yogurt and mix until combined. Store in an airtight container in the fridge for 3 to 4 days.

FRENCH-STYLE "EGG" CANNELLINI SALAD – Makes enough filling for 2 wraps

1 (14½-ounce) can cannellini or other white beans, drained and rinsed (or 1½ cups drained cooked white beans)

8 small gherkins (ensure they are sugar-free), finely chopped

1 shallot, finely chopped

1 teaspoon Dijon mustard

2 tablespoons chopped fresh chives

½ teaspoon kala namak (Indian black salt) or another good-quality salt

Roughly mash the beans with a fork in a bowl. Do not mash them completely; you want to keep some texture. Add the gherkins, shallot, mustard, chives, and kala namak and mix until combined. Store in an airtight container in the fridge for 3 to 4 days.

SERVING SUGGESTIONS:
These bean salads make great fillings for wraps or sandwiches. When making a wrap, it is best to use a large salad leaf (or a bed of smaller greens) between the bean salad and the bread to prevent the bread from becoming soggy. I like to add some grated beet, carrot, thinly sliced cucumber, radishes, alfalfa sprouts, pickled red onions (see page 42), and/or avocado, too. If you want to take the wrap with you for lunch, wrap it in some parchment paper and tie it up.

DAL WITH COCONUT TOPPING

This Indian red lentil dish is one of my daughter's favorite meals (she has a lot of favorites, by the way, and they vary from time to time). There are some spices in here, but it is never too hot or too complex for a child's taste. The coconut topping is a good contrast to the soft lentils and makes this dish even more interesting. So much so that the two-year-old son of some neighbors we invited to dinner was still talking about it the day after he tasted it. It is a perfect introduction to Indian cuisine for children.

Serves 4

2 onions, finely diced

3 garlic cloves, finely diced

1 (1-inch) piece fresh ginger, peeled and finely chopped or grated

1 teaspoon cumin seeds

½ teaspoon coriander seeds

2 teaspoons ground turmeric

½ teaspoon red pepper flakes

1¼ cups red lentils, rinsed

3 to 3¼ cups water or vegetable stock (see page 14)

2½ ounces spinach or chard

½ teaspoon salt, or more to taste

for the topping

¾ cup unsweetened desiccated coconut

1 teaspoon cumin seeds

1 teaspoon coriander seeds

1 teaspoon black mustard seeds (optional)

to serve

3 tablespoons chopped coriander

lemon wedges

Flatbreads (see page 27)

Combine the onions, garlic, and a splash of water or stock in a large nonstick pan. Sauté the onions until they are translucent, 3 to 4 minutes. Add the ginger, spices, and a little more water, if necessary to keep the mixture from burning. Cook for a minute more. Add the lentils to the pan and stir, then pour in the water or stock. Bring to a boil, then reduce the heat to maintain a simmer and cook for about 20 minutes, or until the lentils are cooked. Add the spinach and cook for about 2 minutes more, or until the leaves have wilted. Add the salt.

Meanwhile, make the coconut topping. Toast the coconut and spices in a dry nonstick or cast-iron pan over low heat, stirring frequently. Coconut burns easily, so stay with the pan. When the coconut is golden brown it is ready. Transfer the mixture to a bowl.

Scatter the dal with the coconut topping and serve it with fresh cilantro, lemon wedges, and flatbread alongside.

TIP:
Any leftover dal makes an easy lunch the following day. It is delicious if you pair it with some grains and pickles.

SPINACH CREPES WITH MUSHROOM RAGOUT

French cuisine is not known for being vegan-friendly. That said, the French are widely known for their fine cooking and should not be excluded. One of their more vegan-friendly dishes (though it all depends on the filling) is Brittany's crepe. This crepe is made with buckwheat flour and water, and often has a savory filling. My recipe is a nice twist on the classic dish because I add spinach to the batter. Here the crepe is served with one of its classic toppings: creamy mushrooms. They go so well with the taste of the buckwheat in the crepe.

Serves 4

for the crepes
1⅔ cups buckwheat flour (or use whole-grain)
1½ cups water or plant-based milk
3½ ounces spinach or stemmed kale leaves, washed
1 tablespoon ground linseeds
salt

for the mushroom filling
1 medium onion, finely chopped or sliced
1¾ pounds mixed fresh mushrooms (chanterelle, oyster, or shiitake), cleaned and torn

1 teaspoon fresh thyme leaves
3 garlic cloves, finely chopped
1 teaspoon mushroom powder (see Tip, page 15)
Leaves from ½ small bunch flat-leaf parsley, sage, or oregano, chopped
6 tablespoons Cashew Sour Cream (see page 27 or store-bought nondairy cream
salt and freshly ground black pepper
salad greens, such as arugula, watercress, or baby spinach, to serve

---

Make the crepe batter. Combine all the crepe ingredients in a blender and blend until smooth, or put them in a large bowl and blend using an immersion blender. Set the batter aside to rest for 5 to 10 minutes.

Meanwhile, make the mushroom filling. Heat a nonstick pan. Add the onions and a small splash of water and cook until translucent. Add the fresh mushrooms, thyme, garlic, mushroom powder, and salt and pepper. Cook for 8 to 10 minutes, adding a little more water if needed to prevent burning.

While the mushrooms are cooking, cook the crepes. Heat a 10-inch nonstick pan over medium heat. Pour in 60 to 80ml of the batter and spread it quickly to cover the bottom of the

pan—you want the crepe to be thin. Cook until the surface is dry and the bottom lifts easily from the pan, then flip the crepe over and cook on the second side for a minute or so. (If you flip it too soon, the crepe will break or stick. This is the tricky part of cooking the perfect crepe.) Keep the cooked crepes warm between two plates in the oven on a low temperature. Repeat until all the batter has been used.

When the mushrooms are cooked, taste and adjust the seasoning, if needed. Stir in the fresh herbs and the cashew sour cream until combined.

Spread some mushroom filling over each spinach crepe and fold in half. Serve with a few salad greens. *Bon appétit!*

FIVE-VEGETABLE TAGINE

My French sister-in-law introduced me to a Moroccan-inspired vegetable tagine. The first time she cooked this for me, she used turnips and pumpkin as well as other vegetables. I really liked it and since then it has been part of my repertoire as well. I always use seasonal vegetables for tagine, but feel free to experiment.

Serves 4 to 6

2 red onions, chopped
1¼ cups vegetable stock (see page 14)
1 teaspoon coriander seeds
1 teaspoon cumin seeds
1 cinnamon stick
½ teaspoon ground turmeric
1½ tablespoons harissa paste, plus extra to serve
1 thumb-size piece fresh ginger, peeled and chopped
1 bay leaf
rind of 1 lemon
3 carrots, cut into ¾-inch-thick slices
1 eggplant, chopped into 1-inch chunks

2 medium sweet potatoes, chopped into 1-inch chunks
1 (14-ounce) can tomatoes, chopped
1 (14½-ounce) can chickpeas, drained and rinsed
handful of raisins
salt

to serve
cooked whole-grain couscous, bulgur wheat, or quinoa
3 tablespoons chopped fresh mint
½ cup chopped almonds

Combine the onions with a splash of water or a little of the stock in a large nonstick pan. Sauté the onions until they are soft and translucent, 3 to 4 minutes. Add the coriander, cumin, cinnamon, turmeric, harissa, ginger, bay leaf, lemon rind, carrots, eggplant, and sweet potatoes. Cook, stirring, for 1 minute, adding a few tablespoons of water or stock if needed. Add the remaining stock, the tomatoes, chickpeas, and raisins. Bring to a boil, then reduce the heat to maintain a simmer and cook for 15 to 20 minutes, until the vegetables are soft. Taste and add salt as needed.

Meanwhile, cook the grains according to the instructions on the package.

Serve the tagine with the cooked grains, chopped mint, almonds, and harissa.

GREEN MINESTRONE WITH MARJORAM PESTO

While renovating our home in the depths of winter, we did not have any heat, so I would often make a classic minestrone to keep us warm and energized. The classic version of this soup is made with tomatoes, but when spring comes and the new season's vegetables are available, I feel like having a lighter soup based on fresh greens and herbs.

Serves 4

1 bunch scallions, roughly chopped
5 garlic cloves, chopped
3 celery stalks, chopped
8 cups vegetable stock (see page 14) or water
1½ tablespoons chopped fresh thyme
1 tablespoon chopped fresh rosemary
3 medium potatoes, peeled and diced
1 zucchini, diced
1 fennel bulb, diced
2 teaspoons mushroom powder (see page 15)
1 bay leaf, cracked
7 ounces fava beans (thawed, if frozen)
7 ounces peas (thawed, if frozen)

salt and freshly ground black pepper (optional)

for the pesto
¼ cup pine nuts
⅓ cup walnuts
1 bunch marjoram (or oregano), and chopped
1 bunch basil, chopped
1 garlic clove, chopped
1 avocado, halved, pitted, and chopped
1 tablespoon nutritional yeast
½ teaspoon maple syrup
zest and juice of 1 lemon
salt

Combine the onions, garlic, and celery with a splash of water or a little of the stock in a large nonstick pan. Sauté until the onions are soft and translucent, 3 to 4 minutes. If necessary, add a little more water to prevent burning.

Meanwhile, bring the stock or water to a boil in a separate pan. Add the thyme, rosemary, potatoes, zucchini, fennel, mushroom powder, and bay leaf to the onion mixture, then pour in the hot stock. Bring the stock back to a boil, then reduce the heat to maintain a simmer and cook for 10 minutes. Add the fava beans and cook for

5 minutes more. At the very last minute, add the peas. Taste and add salt and pepper if needed.

While the soup is cooking, make the pesto. Combine all the ingredients in a mortar and mash with the pestle until smooth, or combine in a small food processor and process until smooth. Taste and add salt if needed. The pesto should taste a bit on the salty side, as it will be diluted in the soup.

Serve the soup with a dollop of pesto in each bowl and whole-grain sourdough on the side.

TIP:
This soup freezes very well, so you can make this in advance or make a big batch and freeze in individual portions.

FENNEL AND LEMON STEW

Wild fennel grows abundantly in my garden in France. The moment the fennel flowers or seedheads form, I pick some and start making a recipe with them. Fennel has a distinctive sweet smell and fresh flavor, reminiscent of aniseed and licorice, which I just adore, and it pairs fantastically with lemon. This easy and rustic stew can be made in late summer when the fennel bulbs are just large enough, in autumn, and even in early winter, because both lemons and fennel are still available. These flavors will make you dream of hot and sunny days even when it's cold outside!

Serves 2 as a main or 4 as a side dish

1 pound fennel bulbs

2 bay leaves

3 garlic cloves, crushed

5 lemon slices

1¾ cups vegetable stock (see page 14) or water

14 ounces potatoes (you want a variety that keeps its shape, such as Yukon Gold), sliced

½ teaspoon red pepper flakes, plus more as needed

1 (14-ounce) can fava beans, drained and rinsed (or 1½ cups drained cooked or thawed frozen fava beans)

2½ ounces pitted good-quality black olives, such as Kalamata

3 tablespoons chopped fresh flat-leaf parsley, to serve

Wash the fennel and cut off the stalks (keep the feathery fronds for garnish). Slice the fennel bulbs into thin wedges from top to bottom. Put the slices in a pan with the bay leaves, garlic, lemon, stock, potatoes, and red pepper flakes (adding more red pepper flakes to taste). Bring to a boil, then reduce the heat to maintain a simmer and cook for 15 minutes. Add the fava beans and olives. Simmer for 5 to 7 minutes more, until the fennel is soft and the potatoes are cooked through. Serve garnished with the reserved fennel fronds, parsley, and a few extra red pepper flakes.

TIP:
For a more filling meal, serve the stew with cooked grains, polenta, a nice slice of sourdough, or even whole-grain pasta.

BRUSSELS SPROUT STIR-FRY WITH SPICY PUMPKIN SEEDS

Ask anyone what their least favorite vegetable is, and there is a good chance their answer will be Brussels sprouts. In my opinion, sprouts have this bad reputation because they are often overcooked and then start to smell too strong. But when quickly blanched or stir-fried, sprouts smell less, their texture is crisper, and their taste is far superior. Combined with smoky tofu, the citrus tang of the orange and the earthy tones of the buckwheat, these Brussels sprouts won't disappoint.

Serves 4

for the spicy pumpkin seeds
½ cup raw pumpkin seeds
1 tablespoon maple syrup
½ teaspoon ground chile
1 tablespoon shoyu or tamari

for the stir-fry sauce
juice of 1 orange
3 tablespoons shoyu or tamari
1½ tablespoons balsamic vinegar
1 tablespoon maple syrup
2 teaspoons grated fresh ginger
2 tablespoons water
1 tablespoon cornstarch or arrowroot powder

for the stir-fry
1 leek, trimmed, washed, and thinly sliced
2 carrots, cut into matchsticks, sliced on a
    mandoline, or shredded with a food processor
1 red chile, thinly sliced (seeded, if you want
    less heat), some reserved for garnish
14 ounces Brussels sprouts, thinly sliced on a
    mandoline or shredded with a food processor
4 or 5 garlic cloves, finely chopped
7 ounces smoked tofu, cut into small cubes
    or strips
12 ounces buckwheat noodles or other noodles
    of choice, to serve
small bunch of scallions, finely chopped,
    to serve

Make the spicy pumpkin seeds. Toast the pumpkin seeds in a dry nonstick or cast-iron pan until they start to pop. Stir in the maple syrup and the ground chile and cook for 30 seconds, then stir in the shoyu. Transfer to a sheet of parchment paper, spreading them out into an even layer. Set aside to cool.

Make the stir-fry sauce. Combine all the ingredients for the sauce in a small bowl and set aside.

Heat a wok or a large skillet over high heat (you want to get the pan really hot). Add the leek, carrot, chile and Brussels sprouts and cook, without stirring, until the vegetables begin to brown on the bottom and develop a bit of a crust (you want the vegetables to have a nice caramelized layer, but keep an eye on them so they don't burn), then immediately stir in the garlic and, if needed, a splash of water or stock to prevent burning. Cook, stirring, until the vegetables are cooked but retain some crunch (this should take 2 to 3 minutes from the time you added them to the hot pan). Add the tofu and stir in the sauce. Allow the sauce to thicken - this will take less than a minute.

Cook the noodles according to the package instructions, then rinse and drain. Serve the stir-fried vegetables on the noodles and scatter over the pumpkin seeds, scallions, and the reserved chile.

WINTER TABBOULEH WITH SPICY ZHUG YOGURT SAUCE

Winter produce doesn't have to be dull. Sometimes you just have to be inventive to make seasonal versions of the dishes you like. In summer, tabbouleh would include tomatoes, but who wants to eat out-of-season vegetables that have no flavor? Not me. So I've swapped the tomatoes for grapefruits and added kale to this version.

Serves 4 to 6

for the zhug
5 jalapeños (or 7, if you like extra heat), chopped
1 bunch cilantro, chopped
1 small bunch flat-leaf parsley, chopped
2 or 3 garlic cloves, chopped
¾ teaspoon ground coriander
¾ teaspoon ground cumin
¾ teaspoon ground cardamom
juice of ½ lemon
5 tablespoons natural plant-based yogurt, plus extra to serve, if needed
salt

for the tabbouleh
1½ cups whole-grain buckwheat
¾ cup pumpkin seeds
1 teaspoon coriander seeds
5¼ ounces kale, leaves stemmed and finely shredded or chopped
2 grapefruits, peeled and segmented (catch the juice in a small bowl while segmenting the fruit)
½ bunch mint, finely chopped
1 bunch flat-leaf parsley, finely chopped
¾ cup dried cranberries (ensure they are sugar-free)
salt

Bring 6 cups water to a boil in a large pot.

Make the zhug. Combine all the zhug ingredients in a food processor and process until the mixture has the consistency of pesto. Add salt to taste. If the sauce is too hot, stir some of it into a small bowl of plant-based yogurt. Set aside.

Make the tabbouleh. Add the buckwheat to the boiling water and cook for about 18 minutes—it should retain some bite. Drain in a colander and rinse with cool running water, then drain again.

Meanwhile, toast the pumpkin seeds in a small dry pan over low heat until they start to pop, then transfer to a plate and set aside. In the same pan, toast the coriander seeds until fragrant and set aside on the plate with the pumpkin seeds.

Combine the drained buckwheat, the toasted pumpkin and coriander seeds, the kale, grapefruit segments and juice, mint, parsley, and cranberries in a large bowl. Taste and add more salt if needed. Serve the tabbouleh with the zhug alongside.

TIP:
Winter Tabbouleh is fantastic with the falafel burgers on page 78. It can also be made in advance and will keep for several days in the fridge, and it's great to take to work with you for lunch.

GRILLED AVOCADO WITH RED CHIMICHURRI

Chimichurri is an uncooked sauce that originates from Argentina and Uruguay. There are two versions: one green, *chimichurri verde*, and one red, *chimichurri rojo*. It is often used as a marinade for grilled meat, or is basted onto the meat as it cooks. You can also serve chimichurri as a side dish, as I do here. Here is my recipe for a red chimichurri with avocado, which you can cook on the grill.

Serves 2 as a light lunch or 4 as a starter

for the chimichurri
1 red bell pepper, roughly chopped
2 medium tomatoes, or 9 ounces
  cherry tomatoes
1 small red onion, roughly chopped
½ red chile, seeded and sliced
3 garlic cloves, chopped
1 teaspoon ground cumin
1½ teaspoons dried oregano
1 small bunch cilantro, roughly chopped
1 small bunch flat-leaf parsley, roughly chopped

2 tablespoons raw apple cider vinegar
salt

to serve
2 ripe but still slightly firm avocados, halved
  and pitted
1 (14½-ounce) can pinto or red kidney beans,
  drained and rinsed

Place a grill pan over high heat or heat an outdoor grill to high.

Make the chimichurri. Combine all the ingredients for the chimichurri in a food processor and pulse until the mixture is reasonably smooth (it should still have some texture; it is not meant to be a soup). Transfer the chimichurri to a bowl and set aside.

Place the avocado halves cut-side down on the grill pan or grill grates. Cook for about 3 minutes, or until grill marks appear. Transfer the avocado halves cut-side up to a serving platter or individual plates. Spoon some of the beans into the avocado centers and top with chimichurri Done!

FALAFEL BURGERS WITH TAHINI SAUCE

When I was living in Amsterdam in my early twenties, little falafel shops opened everywhere. I was vegetarian at the time, and it meant I could buy a delicious fast and easy snack just around the corner. If I skipped the yogurt sauce, it was even vegan! Later on I learned about the dangers of deep frying, and because falafel from the shop was fried, I decided to make my own version that I baked in the oven. If your oven has a convection setting, do use it, as it will give your falafel a nice crust without having to use any oil.

Serves 4

For the falafel burgers
2 (14½-ounce) cans chickpeas, drained and
  rinsed (or 3 cups drained cooked chickpeas)
1 bunch flat-leaf parsley, chopped
1 bunch cilantro, chopped
Leaves from ½ bunch mint, chopped
2 teaspoons ground cumin
1 teaspoon ground chile
3 or 4 garlic cloves, chopped
1 teaspoon lemon zest
1 tablespoon fresh lemon juice
1 tablespoon tahini

2 Medjool dates, pitted and roughly chopped
4 to 6 tablespoons chickpea flour or other flour

for the tahini sauce
1 cup tahini
juice of 1½ lemons
½ cup plus 2 tablespoons water (or more,
  depending on how thin you like the sauce)
3 garlic cloves, or less to taste
½ teaspoon ground cumin (optional)
1 teaspoon maple syrup
salt

Preheat the oven to 465°F (or 425°F, if using a convection oven) and line a baking sheet with parchment paper.

Make the falafel burgers. Combine all the burger ingredients except the flour in the bowl of a food processor. Pulse the mixture a few times, then add 4 tablespoons of the flour and pulse until semismooth. To test if the mixture is the right consistency, take a small amount and try to form it into a ball; the mixture should hold its shape. If it is too wet, add the remaining flour; if it's too dry, add 1 or 2 tablespoons water and mix again. The end result should not be completely smooth; it should have some chunks remaining, which gives the burgers more crunch.

Transfer the falafel mixture to a large bowl. Divide the mixture into four equal parts and shape each into a patty with your hands. Transfer them to the lined baking sheet and bake for 18 to 20 minutes in the middle of the oven.

Meanwhile, make the sauce. Combine all the sauce ingredients in a blender. Blend until smooth. Set aside.

Serve the falafels however you like: on flatbread, buns, or whole-grain pitas, with fresh salad greens, sliced radishes, cooked beets, carrot or onion pickles (see page 42), hummus (see page 119), homemade ketchup (see page 22), zhug (see page 75), etc.

TIP:
Both the sauce and the falafel can be stored in separate airtight containers in the fridge for 2 to 3 days. You can also freeze the leftovers and take them out when you need them.

CELERY ROOT SALAD

I have spent many holidays in the Ardèche region of France. Although most tourists go ᵥ
its hot summers, autumn is a lovely season, too, especially when the chestnut harvest ᵇ
Ardèche is justly famous for its chestnuts. In October you can buy them cheaply at the
stalls; I even found local pomegranates on sale then. Sweet chestnuts and crunchy pom
seeds go very well with the nutty, earthy taste of celery root and the bitter radicchio leᵃ
can't get chestnuts, walnuts will work well instead. All flavors are represented here, and
that makes it the perfect autumn salad.

Serves 4

for the dressing
¾ cup Cashew Sour Cream (see page 17)
  or natural plant-based yogurt
1 tablespoon raw apple cider vinegar
2 teaspoons whole-grain mustard
1 garlic clove, finely chopped
½ teaspoon maple syrup
½ teaspoon salt

for the salad
1 cup drained cooked Puy or beluga
  lentils (see page 32)

4 cooked celery root slices (see page 37),
  cut into small cubes
2½ ounces watercress
1 head red radicchio, finely shredded
3½ ounces cooked chestnuts (or walnuts),
  broken up a little
1 small raw Chioggia/candy-striped beet,
  julienned or grated
seeds from 1 pomegranate
1 bunch flat-leaf parsley, roughly chopped

Make the dressing. Combine all the dressing ingredients in a small bowl.

Put the lentils and celery root in a large bowl, pour over the dressing, and stir to combine. Set aside.

Place the watercress and radicchio on a large plate and top with the lentils and celery root. Scatter over the chestnuts, beet, pomegranate seeds, and parsley. Serve as is or, for a more filling meal, with whole-grain sourdough bread, cooked potatoes, or cooked grains.

TIP:
This salad is perfect to take with you for a lunch at your desk. Start by filling a mason jar with the lentils, celery root, and sauce. Add the chestnuts, beet, parsley, and pomegranate seeds. Top with the watercress and red radicchio.

"NO TUNA" SUNFLOWER PÂTÉ IN LETTUCE CUPS

According to the latest research, wild fish in the oceans are rapidly becoming extinct. It is high time to switch to plant-based alternatives, like this fishless "no tuna" pâté made from sunflower seeds.

Serves 4

for the pâté
1 cup sunflower seeds, soaked and drained
8 small gherkins, chopped
2 teaspoons chopped capers
1 small shallot, chopped
1 teaspoon Dijon mustard
1 teaspoon fresh lemon juice
4 to 5 tablespoons natural plant-based yogurt
  or Cashew Sour Cream (see page 17)

for the lettuce cups
1 small head romaine or Little Gem lettuce,
  washed and leaves separated

9 ounces cherry tomatoes, halved (or use
  multicolored tomatoes or the slow-roasted
  tomatoes on page 30)
½ cucumber, sliced into thin rounds
1 red bell pepper, seeded and thinly sliced
2½ ounces pitted black olives, halved
3 tablespoons chopped fresh soft herbs, such
  as flat-leaf parsley, basil, chives, or dill
1 lemon, cut into wedges
salt

Make the pâté. Combine all the pâté ingredients in a food processor and process to a fine texture. Taste and add more salt to your liking; you want it to taste a little salty. Transfer the mixture to a bowl.

Assemble the lettuce cups. Arrange the lettuce leaves on a plate rounded-side down so they form cups. Place a dollop of the pâté inside each leaf. Top with the cherry tomatoes, cucumber, red pepper, and olives. Scatter with the chopped herbs and serve with the lemon wedges alongside to squeeze over the top.

TIPS:
The "no tuna" pâté can easily be made in advance and stored in the fridge for 3 to 4 days. It is very delicious as a "no-tuna melt," sandwiched between two grilled slices of bread with some fresh tomatoes and cashew mozzarella (see page 18). Alternatively, try stirring the "no tuna" pâté into pasta with grated zucchini and blanched peas for a great, super-simple dinner.

CUP-A-NOODLES

Instant noodles can be bought in many Asian stores in Holland, as in most parts of the world. I used to buy them and enjoy them as a quick snack. It's so easy: put the noodles in hot water and then add the little spice packet for flavor. There's even a vegetarian version—but that doesn't mean it's healthy. After all, it's just some dried noodles with a spice bag packed with lots of salt, E-numbers, and additives. Far better to make your own soup! In this recipe, I use the umami paste from the Weekends chapter as the flavor base, and I've added lots of fresh vegetables to make this a delicious and healthy soup.

Serves 2

3½ ounces noodles of choice
1 sweet potato, spiralized, sliced with
  a julienne cutter, or shaved into ribbons
  with a vegetable peeler
1 zucchini, spiralized, sliced with
  a julienne cutter, or shaved into ribbons
  with a vegetable peeler
vegetables of choice (sugar snap peas, cooked

broccoli, bean sprouts, finely sliced bok choy,
  radish slices
sliced fresh chile
2 teaspoons grated fresh ginger
2 tablespoons chopped fresh herbs, such as
  cilantro, chives, or Thai basil
2 tablespoons Umami Paste (see page 15),
  or more to taste

Cook the noodles according to the package instructions until al dente (not mushy). Drain and rinse the noodles, then divide them between two bowls or heatproof glass jars. Divide the sweet potato, zucchini, vegetables, chile, ginger, and herbs between the jars as well. Top each one with 1 tablespoon of the umami paste. Pour over 2 cups hot water (this will dissolve the umami paste), and your healthy cup of noodles is ready!

SUMMER TOMATO TART WITH HERBED AVOCADO CREAM

In the height of summer, whenever I'm in France, every Tuesday morning I go to the "pick your own" garden in the next village to get the most beautiful and tasty varieties of tomatoes. The garden is closed on Sundays and Mondays, so I have to be quick on Tuesdays; otherwise, all the fresh tomatoes will go and there won't be anything left to use to make this tart—it's the perfect thing to eat on a hot day!

Serves 4

for the tart
2 tablespoons ground chia seeds or flaxseed
1¾ cups almond flour
100g fine oat flakes
½ teaspoon salt
1 pound tomatoes (preferably different colors),
  sliced horizontally
smoked coarse sea salt, to serve

for the avocado cream
2 medium avocados, halved and pitted
2 garlic cloves, finely chopped
1 large bunch basil or tarragon (or a mix)
1 tablespoon fresh lemon juice
½ teaspoon chopped red chile (optional)
salt

Preheat the oven to 400°F and line the bottom of a 9-inch round or 5 x 14-inch rectangular tart pan with a removable bottom with parchment paper.

Mix the chia seeds with ¼ cup water in a large bowl and let sit for 5 minutes so the seeds absorb the water. They will form an egg-like consistency to bind the ingredients together.

Add the almond flour, oat flakes, and salt to the chia seed mixture and mix with a fork to combine. Using your hands, form the mixture into a ball. Using your fingers, press the crust into an even, not-too-thick layer over the bottom and up the sides of the lined tart pan. Transfer the pan to the oven and bake for 12 to 15 minutes, until the crust is light golden brown and there is a small gap between the crust and the pan. Remove from the oven and let cool slightly (it doesn't need long; 2 minutes is enough).

Meanwhile, make the herbed avocado cream. Combine all the ingredients in a food processor or blender and process until smooth. Taste and season with salt as needed.

When the crust has cooled, spread the avocado cream evenly over the bottom of the crust, then arrange the tomatoes on top, overlapping them slightly. Gently remove the tart from the pan and sprinkle over the coarse sea salt before serving with a green salad.

AUTUMN BOWLS WITH BALSAMIC REDUCTION

Using some roasted or cooked vegetables, cooked grains (prepped over the weekend), or leftovers from the days before, you can make these vegetable bowls as a super-quick weekday meal. This one is a fine example of a bowl that I like to make.

Serves 4

1 cup tricolor quinoa (or use 4 cups cooked grains)
1 teaspoon fennel seeds
4 ripe tomatoes (heirloom, if you can find them), sliced into wedges
4 fresh figs, quartered
1 pound roasted pumpkin or cooked beets (see page 53)
leaves from 1 bunch fresh herbs, such as tarragon or basil, torn
salt and freshly ground black pepper

Cashew Mozzarella (see page 18) or
1 (14½-ounce) can white beans, such as cannellini or butter beans, drained and rinsed (or 1½ cups drained cooked white beans)

for the balsamic reduction
1 cup balsamic vinegar
¼ cup maple syrup
sprigs of fresh thyme, washed

Unless you are using precooked quinoa (or another cooked grain), cook it according to the instructions on the package.

Meanwhile, make the balsamic reduction. Put the ingredients for the balsamic reduce in a small pan and bring to a gentle boil. Reduce the heat to maintain a simmer and cook for 10 to 15 minutes, until the mixture has reduced by one-third. Set aside to cool.

Toast the fennel seeds in a dry nonstick or cast-iron pan over low heat, moving the seeds around so they don't burn, until they start to smell fragrant, about 2 minutes. Transfer the seeds to a mortar and crush them using the pestle

(Alternatively, grind them in a spice grinder or crush them using a rolling pin). Tip the seeds into a medium bowl and add the tomatoes, figs, and salt and pepper to taste. Set aside.

Now you can assemble your autumn bowls. Start layering by adding some cooked quinoa to your bowl, then the roasted pumpkin or cooked beet. Continue by adding the prepared tomato-fig mixture to your bowls. If you are using the cashew mozzarella or beans, add them now. Scatter over the fresh herbs and serve drizzled with the balsamic reduction.

TIP:
This salad can easily be taken with you, in which case, put the balsamic reduction in a separate container and pour it over the salad just before eating.

CREAMY NO-RECIPE PASTA

I could call this "recipe" all sorts of things, but I won't. Let's just say it is a good and delicious pasta that hasn't got a real recipe. The base is always the same. With the addition of my cashew sour cream, you get a really lovely creamy pasta sauce. Furthermore, I add whatever I have in my fridge, freezer, or cupboard. Follow the basic recipe and use one of the add-ins that I suggest. When you are confident enough, just improvise and make this your own.

Serves 4

2 cups Cashew Sour Cream (see page 17; either version is fine)
5 tablespoons nutritional yeast
juice of ½ lemon
3 garlic cloves, finely chopped
12 to 14 ounces whole-grain pasta (or gluten-free pasta, if you prefer)
salt and freshly ground black pepper

Suggested add-ins:

1 serving Slow-Roasted Cherry Tomatoes (see page 30) and 2½ ounces chopped arugula or spinach

7 ounces thawed peas or cooked fava beans; 1 small bunch basil, flat-leaf parsley, tarragon, or oregano, chopped; and 1 tablespoon chopped fresh red chile

1 head broccoli, divided into florets and cooked; zest of 1 lemon; 2 tablespoons pine nuts, toasted; and a dash of ground chile

Roast Pumpkin (see page 53), a grating of nutmeg, 2 tablespoons chopped fresh flat-leaf parsley or sage, and a dash of ground chile

1 cup sautéed mushrooms of choice, 1 tablespoon mushroom powder (see Tip, page 15), and a small handful of chopped fresh soft herbs, such as flat-leaf parsley, oregano, or chives

Bring a large pot of water to a boil for the pasta.

Meanwhile, in a bowl, mix together the cashew sour cream, nutritional yeast, lemon juice, garlic, and salt and pepper. Set aside.

When the water boils, cook the pasta according to the instructions on the package. Reserve some of the cooking liquid, then drain the pasta.

Combine the drained pasta with the cashew sour cream mixture and your chosen add-ins. If the sauce is too thick, stir in a bit of the reserved pasta cooking liquid. Serve hot.

CARROT AND ZUCCHINI FRITTERS WITH ITALIAN SALSA VERDE

Making a vegetable the star of my meal is mostly what I do. Where traditional menus always focus on the meat, I focus on the greens. I use what I have in my home and what is in season. I always have carrots, because they are so versatile: you can eat them raw as a snack, make juice, use them in a stir fry, use them in soups or you can add them to a plant-based burger. Here I make carrots into fritters. They are not difficult to make, and you can eat any leftovers as a quick snack, add them to a salad, or serve them in a wrap the next day. I have paired the sweet flavor of the carrot with a flavorful Italian salsa verde. *Buon appetito!*

Makes about 10

4 medium carrots, coarsely grated
1 medium zucchini, coarsely grated
1 teaspoon salt
1⅔ cups chickpea flour or whole-grain flour
good pinch of ground chile
2 teaspoons dried thyme
zest of 1 lemon
3 tablespoons chopped flat-leaf parsley

for the salsa verde
1 large bunch flat-leaf parsley, roughly chopped
juice of ½ lemon
1 or 2 garlic cloves, finely chopped
1 tablespoon chopped capers
1½ teaspoons Dijon mustard
2 to 3 tablespoons natural plant-based yogurt

Combine the grated carrots and zucchini with the salt in a colander and set in the sink for 5 minutes to release their water. Place them between a couple of sheets of paper towels and squeeze out excess moisture.

Combine the flour, ground chile, thyme, lemon zest, parsley, and ½ cup plus 2 tablespoons water in a large bowl. Mix until there are no clumps. Add the grated vegetables and stir to coat them with the batter.

Heat a nonstick pan over medium heat, drop 2 to 3 tablespoons of the fritter batter into the pan and press it down to form a patty. Cook for 5 to 7 minutes on one side, until the top starts to look dry and small bubbles appear. Flip the fritter and cook for 5 to 7 minutes more. Transfer the cooked fritter to a plate and keep warm in a low oven. Repeat until all the fritter batter has been used.

While the fritters are cooking, make the salsa verde. Combine all the salsa verde ingredients in a small food processor and pulse until the mixture has the consistency of a pesto. Transfer the salsa verde to a small bowl.

Serve the fritters with the salsa verde and some salad greens, such as watercress.

URAP-URAP WITH KECAP SAUCE AND SAMBAL

Part of Dutch culture is influenced by one of its former colonies, Indonesia, and Indonesians who have settled in the Netherlands have enriched our food culture in ways we couldn't imagine before. Dishes such as *nasi*, *bami*, and *saté* are now so famous in Holland that almost everyone eats them once a week. *Urap-urap* is less well-known, but equally delicious. It is a traditional steamed vegetable salad with a spiced and grated coconut topping. There are a few components to this dish and you may think this is a lot of work, but in fact your kitchen equipment does most of it. Allow this dish to sweep you off your feet and leave your guests impressed!

Serves 4

1½ cups whole-grain rice (for this dish, I like red rice)

14 ounces green beans, trimmed and sliced into 1½- to 2-inch pieces

10½ ounces cavolo nero, kale, or savoy cabbage, central ribs removed, leaves cut into bite-size pieces

1½ cups bean sprouts

for the sambal (hot chile sauce)

3½ ounces fresh chiles, roughly chopped

2 or 3 garlic cloves, finely chopped

1 small red onion or shallot, diced

1 (1-inch) piece fresh ginger, peeled and chopped

juice of ½ lemon, or 2 tablespoons raw apple cider vinegar

2 tablespoons shoyu or tamari

for the kecap sauce

scant ½ cup shoyu or tamari

scant ½ cup maple syrup

½ red chile, sliced

2 star anise pods

3 garlic cloves, crushed

3 slices fresh ginger

1½ teaspoons cornstarch or arrowroot, mixed with 1 tablespoon water

for the coconut topping

1 shallot, finely diced

4 garlic cloves, finely chopped

½ red chile, seeded and finely chopped (or use 1 teaspoon of the sambal)

1 cup unsweetened desiccated coconut

1 teaspoon ground turmeric

1 teaspoon ground coriander

1 tablespoon maple syrup or coconut sugar

1 tablespoon shoyu or tamari

Rinse and cook the rice according to the package instructions.

Make the sambal. Combine all the ingredients for the sambal in a food processor (you might want to wear gloves for handling the chiles) and pulse until the mixture has a smooth, sauce-like consistency. Transfer the sambal to a small jar or bowl and set aside.

Make the kecap sauce. Combine all the ingredients except the cornstarch in a small pan over low heat. Bring to a gentle boil, stirring, then reduce the heat to low and cook until the sauce has reduced and thickened, 10 to 15 minutes. Stir in the cornstarch mixture and cook to thicken the sauce a little more, less than a minute. Pour the sauce into a small bowl and set aside.

continued

⟶ Make the coconut topping. Combine the shallot, garlic, and chile (or sambal) in a nonstick or cast-iron pan. Add a splash of water and cook over medium-high heat until the shallot is soft and lightly golden. Add the desiccated coconut, turmeric, and coriander to the pan and cook, stirring often, until the texture of the mixture is more dry than liquid, like a crumble, and the coconut is golden brown. (Desiccated coconut will burn quickly, so be sure to stir often.) Add the maple syrup and shoyu, give it a good stir, and cook, stirring continuously, for a minute more.

While the topping cooks, steam the vegetables. Bring a large pan of water to a boil and set a steamer on top. Put the green beans in the steamer—they will take the longest—and cook for

5 to 6 minutes, then add the kale and cook for 2 to 3 minutes more. Add the bean sprouts for the final minute of cooking—you don't want the vegetables to be overcooked, so keep an eye on them and taste to check whether they are ready. The beans should be cooked through but still have a light crunch.

When the vegetables are ready, combine them with the coconut topping. Serve with the rice, sambal, and kecap sauce. Enjoy your meal—or selamat makan, as they say in Indonesia!

CHIA PUDDING FOR ALL SEASONS

This pudding is easy to make in advance and it lasts up to five days in the fridge. It is adaptable to every season if you use different fruit toppings. You can add different spices, too. On days when you are really hungry, you can add your favorite granola (see page 102) to make it even more fulfilling. A very versatile pudding, indeed!

Serves 4 (makes about 4 cups)

1 cup black or white chia seeds
4 cups nut milk or other plant-based milk
scant ½ cup of your preferred liquid sweetener
   (maple syrup, brown rice syrup, or coconut
   nectar)

¾ teaspoon vanilla powder
pinch of good-quality salt

Put the chia seeds in a large bowl or container such as a mason jar. Stir in the milk, sweetener, vanilla powder, and salt. Stir well or, if the container has a lid, close the lid and shake for 10 to 15 minutes for the chia seeds to soak up all the ingredients. Shake or stir every 5 minutes to ensure the seeds really absorb all the milk.

ADDITIONAL SPICES YOU CAN ADD TO THE BASIC RECIPE:

for a Golden Turmeric Pudding, add:
2 teaspoons ground turmeric, 1 teaspoon ground ginger, 1 teaspoon ground cinnamon, and a few grinds of black pepper

for a Decadent Pudding add:
6 tablespoons carob or cacao powder

for a Chai Pudding, add:
1 tablespoon carob or cacao powder, 1½ teaspoons ground cinnamon, ¾ teaspoon ground ginger, pinch of freshly grated nutmeg, and ½ teaspoon ground cardamom

FRUIT COMBINATIONS TO USE AS A TOPPING FOR YOUR CHIA PUDDING:

- 9 ounces pitted apricots, sliced or cubed, combined with 4½ ounces raspberries, 4½ ounces blueberries, a handful of chopped unsalted pistachio nuts, and 1 teaspoon orange blossom water (optional)
- 9 ounces pitted plums, sliced; 4½ ounces blackberries; 1 pear, cored and cubed or sliced; ½ teaspoon ground cardamom; and a handful of chopped walnuts
- 2 blood oranges, peeled and cut into slices or segments; 5 Medjool dates, pitted and sliced; seeds of 1 pomegranate; and ½ teaspoon ground cinnamon

continued ⎯⎯⎯⎯⎯⎯⟶

—→ ADD THIS RHUBARB AND STRAWBERRY COMPOTE FOR A SPRING VERSION OF CHIA PUDDING:

9 ounces rhubarb, chopped into 1-inch pieces
9 ounces strawberries, hulled (reserve a few for decoration)
juice of 1 orange

¼ cup brown rice syrup
1½ teaspoons rose water (optional)
1½ teaspoons cornstarch or arrowroot powder, blended with 2 tablespoons water

Combine all the ingredients except the cornstarch in a pan and bring to a boil over medium-low heat. Once the fruits start to release their juices and the liquid starts to bubble, reduce the heat to maintain a simmer and cook for 5 to 7 minutes. Taste to check whether the compote needs additional sweetener. Stir in the cornstarch mixture and allow the compote to thicken, about 1 minute. Let cool completely, then transfer to a jar or other airtight container and store in the fridge. Serve this on top of your chia pudding.

TIP:
If you put the chia pudding and the fruit topping in a mason jar, you can easily take it to work with you.

NO TIME
AT ALL

There are no excuses not to eat healthy food even
when you are in hurry, whether it's breakfast,
lunch, or dinnertime. That doesn't mean you just
have to grab a snack, either. In this chapter I will
show you that within 15 minutes, you can have a
delicious and healthy meal. For breakfast, try my
granola or smoothie bowl; for lunch, there's my
chickpea shawarma; and in the evening, you can
enjoy a classic meal like pasta, pizza, or curry.
It's all here!

SPEEDY CHEAT'S NUT MILK

This speedy nut milk is the answer if you are out of store-bought plant-based milk. It calls for just three ingredients and a blender. Once you have tried the basic recipe, you can make it your own by adding other ingredients, such as vanilla, cinnamon, or cacao or carob powder.

Makes 2 cups

3 tablespoons nut butter (almond, cashew, peanut butter, etc.)

pinch of salt (only if you are using a pure nut butter without added salt)

Combine the nut butter, salt (if using), and 2 cups water in a blender and blend until a "milk" forms. Use immediately, or transfer to a jar and store in the refrigerator to use within 24 hours.

SMOOTHIE BOWL

If you've seen all the Instagram pictures of smoothie bowls, you might think no one eats anything else. But perhaps these smoothie lovers are right. A smoothie makes a wonderful light breakfast and a great dessert, one that can be made in no time. All you need are frozen berries, a blender, and your phone ready to take a nice picture and join the #smoothiebowl hashtag!

Serves 2 or 3

4½ ounces frozen raspberries
4½ ounces frozen strawberries
4½ ounces frozen blueberries (I like wild ones)
3 bananas
½ cup plus 2 tablespoons nut milk of choice
1 teaspoon lemon or lime juice

½ teaspoon vanilla powder
2 Medjool dates, pitted

to serve
fresh fruit of choice
chopped nuts of choice

Combine the frozen berries, bananas, nut milk, lemon juice, vanilla powder, and dates in a high-speed blender and blend until smooth. Pour into two or three bowls and serve topped with fresh fruit and chopped nuts.

BREAKFAST POLENTA (SWEET AND SAVORY)

When the temperature outside drops below 55°F, there is only one breakfast I really start to crave: a wholesome bowl of soothing and warming porridge. All kinds of grains, including pseudograins like buckwheat and rolled grains, can be prepared as a porridge. This particular one is made from polenta. Use quick-cook polenta, as it cooks in minutes (traditional polenta can take up to 40 minutes, so check the label before you buy it).

SWEET POLENTA PORRIDGE – Serves 2 or 3

½ cup quick-cook polenta

2½ cups almond milk (you can use the Speedy
  Cheat's Milk on page 98)

½ teaspoon vanilla powder

½ teaspoon ground allspice

½ teaspoon ground cinnamon, plus extra
  to serve

¼ cup maple syrup or brown rice syrup

to serve

sliced fruits, such as pineapple, banana,
  mangos, and/or dates

coconut yogurt

chopped fresh mint

Combine the polenta and the almond milk in a pan and cook, stirring with a whisk, until the mixture comes to a boil and starts to thicken. Reduce the heat to medium-low and add the vanilla, allspice, cinnamon, and maple syrup. Cook, stirring occasionally, for 5 to 7 minutes. Pour into bowls and serve topped with fruits, yogurt, chopped mint, and cinnamon.

SAVORY POLENTA – Serves 2 or 3

½ cup quick-cook polenta

2½ cups almond milk

1 teaspoon dried oregano

1 tablespoon nutritional yeast

½ teaspoon salt, plus more if needed

2 large handfuls of greens, such as kale,
  Swiss chard, or spring greens, stemmed
  and very thinly sliced

9 ounces fresh or Slow-Roasted Cherry
  Tomatoes (see page 30)

small handful of fresh soft herbs, such as basil,
  tarragon, parsley, or chives

Savory Toppings (see pages 24–25) or
  chopped nuts of your choice

red pepper flakes

Combine the polenta and the almond milk in a pan and cook, stirring with a whisk, until the mixture comes to a boil and starts to thicken. Reduce the heat to medium-low and add the oregano, nutritional yeast, and salt. Cook, stirring from time to time, for 3 minutes. Add the greens and cook for 2 to 3 minutes more. Taste to see if it needs a bit more salt and adjust accordingly. Remove from the heat. Pour into two or three bowls and serve topped with the tomatoes, chopped herbs, savory topping or nuts, and a touch of red pepper flakes.

STOVETOP GRANOLA

Did you ever get a package of granola from a shop and look at the ingredients and the price? Well, I did. Call me Dutch, but if you make your own granola, it is far less expensive and has no refined sugars, trans-fats, or other questionable things; and, best of all, you can put in the things you love. And by cooking the granola in a pan on the stovetop, you can make it in minutes. So no excuses—this recipe will have you creating your own in no time. I am sure you are going to love making and eating it.

Makes 5 servings

1⅔ cups rolled oats
5 tablespoons sunflower seeds

5 tablespoons pumpkin seeds
¼ cup maple syrup

Toast the oats and seeds in a cast-iron or nonstick pan over medium heat, stirring frequently to prevent burning, until the oats turn golden and fragrant and the seeds start to pop, 6 to 8 minutes.

Remove from the heat and add the maple syrup to the hot pan. Stir quickly to coat with the syrup, then spread over a sheet of parchment paper to cool down. If you want to add some dried fruit (about ½ cup), this is the time.

Once cooled (this will take just 2 minutes or so), it's ready to eat. This granola is good served with some speedy cheat's nut milk (see page 98), plant-based yogurt, or some seasonal fruits (or a mix of these).

The granola will keep in an airtight container at room temperature for 10 to 14 days.

INDIAN-STYLE TOFU SCRAMBLE WITH QUICK MANGO CHUTNEY

Most people who start eating a plant-based diet don't really understand tofu, finding it bland and lacking in flavor. I must admit that they are right, but, as with chicken or cauliflower, which are also bland, you have to add the flavors you love. Consider tofu a vehicle for many different flavors. I am sure the Indian spices in this dish, paired with the chutney, will change the mind of any "tofu doubter."

Serves 2

for the scramble
½ teaspoon black mustard seeds
¼ teaspoon cumin seeds
¼ teaspoon coriander seeds
5¼ ounces cherry tomatoes, quartered (you can also use cooked sweet potato or pumpkin chunks)
1 teaspoon curry powder
4 scallions, chopped into ½-inch pieces
9 ounces medium-firm tofu, drained and mashed with a fork to the consistency of scrambled egg
2 handfuls of washed spinach (about 3½ ounces)
1 green chile, sliced (seeded, if you like it less hot)

kala namak (Indian black salt), if you can find it, or another good-quality salt

for the chutney (makes a large jar)
½ teaspoon cumin seeds
2 mangoes, halved and cubed
1 thumb-size piece fresh ginger, peeled and chopped
½ teaspoon red ground chile (for less heat, use ¼ teaspoon)
½ teaspoon ground cardamom
1 tablespoon raw apple cider vinegar
2 Medjool dates, pitted and chopped
½ red onion, chopped
salt

Make the chutney. Toast the cumin seeds in a cast-iron pan over low heat for just 30 seconds or so, until the seeds start to smell fragrant. Set aside on a plate to cool (keep the pan nearby, as you'll use it for the scramble). If you have a mortar and pestle, grind the seeds. If not, it's fine to leave them whole.

Combine the mango cubes, toasted cumin, ginger, red ground chile, cardamom, vinegar, dates, and onion in a high-speed blender and blend until smooth. Taste and add salt to your liking. Set aside.

Make the scramble. In the same pan you used earlier, toast the mustard, cumin, and coriander seeds until fragrant. Add the cherry tomatoes, curry powder, and onions and increase the heat to medium-high. If needed, add a splash of water to prevent burning. Cook, stirring, for about 3 minutes, or until the onions and tomatoes have softened. Add the tofu and spinach and mix well. Cook until the spinach has wilted. Top with the green chile and season with salt to taste.

Serve the scramble with the chutney, some flatbread (see page 27), and pickled onion (see page 42).

VEGAN PASTA PUTTANESCA

There are many stories surrounding the origin of this dish, largely due to its name, which some sources say refers to ladies of the night. But one thing is sure: this pasta is packed with flavor. It's salty because of the capers and olives, hot from the chile, and fragrant from the garlic. A real mix of great tastes!

Serves 4

14 ounces pasta of your choice (spelt, whole-grain, gluten-free, etc.)

for the sauce
1 red onion, chopped
1 pound cherry tomatoes, quartered (or if you are in a real hurry, use 10½ ounces Slow-Roasted Cherry Tomatoes; see page 30)
5 garlic cloves, chopped

½ teaspoon (or more) ground chile or red pepper flakes
2 teaspoons drained capers, roughly chopped
2½ ounces good-quality black olives, such as Kalamata, drained and roughly chopped
salt (optional)

to serve
2 tablespoons chopped fresh flat-leaf parsley
Nut Parmesan (see page 26)

Bring a large pan of water to a boil for the pasta.

Make the sauce. Starting with a dry pan, cook the onion in a large nonstick skillet over high heat. When the onion begins to caramelize, add a little water to deglaze the pan (if you use too much water, the onion will steam and not fry, so use it sparingly). Cook the onion for 3 to 5 minutes, until golden and soft. Add the tomatoes and garlic to the pan. Cook for about 2 minutes, then add the chile, capers, and olives. Reduce the heat to medium and cook for 6 to 8 minutes

more, adding a little more water if needed to ensure the sauce doesn't burn. Taste and add salt if needed (remember, the olives and capers are very salty).

Meanwhile, cook the pasta in the boiling water according to the package instructions. Reserve some of the pasta cooking water, then drain the pasta and add it to the sauce. If needed, add a splash of the reserved cooking water to loosen the sauce slightly. Serve with the parsley and some nut parmesan.

PASTA WITH ZUCCHINI, WHITE BEANS, AND GRILLED LEMON

Pasta is one of those simple, fast meals, and is always a crowd-pleaser. This summery pasta dish is a perfect example of lazy cooking with maximum results.

Serves 4

2 tablespoons pine nuts
2 lemons, halved
12 to 14 ounces pasta of your choice (spelt, whole-grain, gluten-free, etc.)
1 (14½-ounce) can white beans, such as cannellini, drained and rinsed (or 1½ cups drained cooked white beans)

2 zucchini (yellow, green, or both), coarsely grated
1 or 2 garlic cloves, finely chopped
3 to 4 tablespoons Cashew Sour Cream (see page 17) or natural plant-based yogurt
leaves from ½ bunch mint, chopped
salt and red pepper flakes

Bring a large pan of water to a boil for the pasta. Toast the pine nuts in a dry pan over low heat until golden brown. Set them aside on a plate.

Heat a cast-iron grill pan. Place the lemons cut-side down on the hot pan and cook until grill marks appear. Set aside.

Cook the pasta in the boiling water according to the package instructions. During the last minute of cooking, add the beans to the pot to cook with the pasta. Reserve some of the pasta cooking liquid (a small cup will do), then drain the pasta and beans and return them to the same pan or transfer them to a large bowl.

Add the grated zucchini, garlic, cashew cream, and salt and red pepper flakes to taste. Stir in some of the reserved cooking liquid to loosen the mixture slightly. Serve the pasta topped with the fresh mint, grilled lemon halves, and toasted pine nuts.

PIZZA COMING UP!

Pizza: What's not to love about it? It is one of the most famous foods in the world, and is often sold frozen. When time is lacking, people tend to throw a store-bought frozen pizza in the oven for a quick meal. They forget (sometimes deliberately) that it can be filled with fats, calories, and salt. I think this meal can be so much better, and with flatbreads you have an ideal pizza base. If you make flatbreads over the weekend and have some tomato sauce left from another meal, you are nearly there. You just need a topping. I use figs, mozzarella, and arugula as toppings in this recipe. But don't be afraid to experiment—use whatever is in your fridge. The key to a great pizza? A hot oven and good-quality ingredients. You're never going back to frozen pizza again!

Makes 2 pizzas

2 whole-grain flatbreads, homemade
 (see page 27) or store-bought
1 serving tomato sauce, homemade
 (see page 30) or good-quality jarred sauce
3 fresh figs, cut into rounds

a couple of balls of homemade Cashew
 Mozzarella (see page 18), sliced
5 tablespoons pine nuts
splash of good-quality balsamic vinegar
2½ ounces arugula

Preheat the oven to its highest setting.

On each flatbread, spread 3 tablespoons tomato sauce and top with the figs, mozzarella, pine nuts, and vinegar.

If possible, place both pizzas in the middle of the hot oven; if not, cook them one at a time. Bake for 4 to 5 minutes, until the bottom is crispy. Remove from the oven and scatter over some arugula for extra punch. Now eat!

MEXICAN BLACK BEAN SALAD WITH JALAPEÑO CREMA

Beans are one of the staple ingredients in my vegan kitchen—and for good reason. They are high in protein, minerals, and fiber; low in fat; and very cheap. They are a mainstay in many traditional food cultures. Think of Indian dal, a daily meal for millions; stews and soups from Italy (people in Tuscany were often referred to as *mangiafagioli* or "bean eaters"); and the chiles and mashed refried beans of Mexico. In this Mexican-inspired dish, the beans are not mashed, but instead treated as croutons; the black beans have a crisp outside and are flavored with Mexican spices.

Serves 4

for the salad
kernels from 2 fresh ears corn
1 head romaine or 2 small Little Gem lettuces, washed and leaves separated
9 ounces various colored tomatoes, sliced (or halved, if you use tiny ones)
leaves from small bunch cilantro
1 (14½-ounce) can black beans, drained and rinsed (or 1½ cups drained cooked black beans)
1½ teaspoons paprika
½ teaspoon ground chile

1½ teaspoons dried oregano
1 teaspoon ground cumin
½ teaspoon garlic granules
salt

for the jalapeño crema
1 cup natural plant-based yogurt
1 avocado, pitted and peeled
1 jalapeño, seeded and sliced, or 1½ to 2 tablespoons pickled jalapeño
juice of 1 lime
1 small garlic clove, chopped

Bring a medium pan of water to a boil. Add the corn kernels and cook for 2 minutes, then drain and set aside.

Make the jalapeño crema. Combine all the crema ingredients in a blender (or in a medium bowl, if using an immersion blender) and blend until smooth. Taste and add salt as needed. Pour the crema into a bowl (if you used a standard blender) and set aside.

Arrange the salad leaves, tomatoes, corn kernels, and cilantro leaves on a large plate and set aside.

Put the beans and all the spices in a bowl and stir to coat the beans with the spices. Add salt to taste. Heat a dry pan over medium-high heat and add the spicy beans. They will quickly become dry and start to break up or pop—this is fine. Cook, shaking the pan so the beans don't burn, until heated through but not overly hot. Scatter the beans on top of the salad and serve with the jalapeño crema.

SUPER-FAST THAI BLENDER CURRY

Thai food is the perfect cuisine for those moments when you need a tasty meal but time is short. Thai dishes are based on quick cooking techniques using fresh, aromatic, and spicy ingredients. By making a curry in a blender, you save time and still get a great meal that is super delicious and packed with goodness.

Serves 4

3 scallions, chopped
1 thumb-size piece fresh ginger, roughly
  chopped
juice of 1 lime
1 bunch cilantro, roughly chopped (reserve a
  few leaves for garnish)
3 garlic cloves, crushed
2 tablespoons coconut sugar
1½ tablespoons shoyu, tamari, or Umami Paste
  (see page 15)
1 red or green chile (more if you like it hot),
  plus extra to serve

1⅔ cups coconut milk
½ cup vegetable stock (see page 14) or water
1 head broccoli, cut into florets, stem
  peeled and sliced, or 10½ ounces
  Broccolini
1 zucchini, halved lengthwise and cut into half-
  moons
7 ounces snow peas, halved
¾ cup raw cashews
2 limes, cut into wedges
salt
cooked whole-grain rice or noodles, to serve

Preheat the oven to 350°F and line a baking sheet with parchment paper.

Combine the scallions, ginger, lime juice, cilantro, garlic, coconut sugar, shoyu, tamari, chile, coconut milk, and stock in a blender and blend until smooth. Pour the mixture into a large pan and bring to a boil. Add the broccoli and zucchini, reduce the heat to medium, and cook for 4 to 5 minutes Add the snow peas. Cook for 3 to 4 minutes more, until the vegetables are cooked through but still have some bite—you don't want to overcook them. Taste the curry and add salt if needed.

Meawhile, put the cashews on the lined baking sheet and bake in the middle of the oven for 4 minutes. Stir the cashews and cook them for 3 to 5 minutes more, until golden. The nuts can burn easily, so check them frequently. Remove from the oven and let them cool a little, then roughly chop them.

Top the curry with the chopped cashews, wedges of lime, reserved cilantro leaves, and some chopped chile for additional heat, if you like. Serve with some cooked whole-grain rice or noodles.

ASIAN SALAD WITH TEMPEH

Tempeh is an Indonesian product made from fermented soy beans. Chopped finely or even grated, it makes a wonderful alternative to ground beef—so good, in fact, that you can easily fool a big meat lover.

Serves 4

9 ounces tempeh

9 ounces mung bean or rice noodles

7 ounces peas

handful of sugar snap peas or snow peas, halved

1 teaspoon garlic granules

1 tablespoon maple syrup

3 tablespoons water

1 red chile, seeded and finely chopped

1 teaspoon Chinese five-spice powder

1 tablespoon rice vinegar or balsamic vinegar

¼ cup soy sauce or tamari

½ small napa cabbage, shredded

1 zucchini, spiralised or cut with a julienne cutter

½ bunch of scallions, finely chopped

for the sauce

¼ cup soy sauce or tamari

¼ cup water

1 tablespoon rice vinegar or balsamic vinegar

1 teaspoon grated fresh ginger

1 teaspoon maple syrup

1 tablespoon tahini

red pepper flakes

Bring a large pan of water to a boil. Add the noodles and cook according to the package instructions. During the last minute of cooking, add the peas and sugar snaps. Drain and rinse under cold running water, then drain again.

Meanwhile, put the tempeh in a food processor and pulse until it has broken down to a crumbly consistency. Transfer the tempeh to a hot, dry pan. Stir-fry the tempeh while adding the garlic, maple syrup, water, chile, five-spice powder, vinegar, and soy sauce. Cook for 4 to 5 minutes,

adding a splash of water if needed to prevent burning. Set aside.

Make the sauce. Combine all the sauce ingredients in a small bowl.

Tip the noodles into a large bowl or onto a serving plate. Add the napa cabbage, peas, zucchini, and scallions and toss to combine with the noodles. Add the tempeh, drizzle the sauce over the top, and serve.

TIP:
For extra crunch, use the Almond and Sesame Topping on page 24.

JAPANESE-STYLE GRILLED EGGPLANT WITH SWEET-AND-SOUR CUCUMBER

As soon as August comes, I start looking forward to getting young fresh eggplant from a "pick your own" near my home in France. They are grown in glasshouses and are quite hard to harvest since the stems have small spikes. Aubergines are often baked or grilled while drenched in oil, but instead of using a lot of oil, I prefer to steam the eggplant and then add flavorings to them. The umami paste from the Weekends chapter (see page 15) gives this dish a Japanese touch. The tart cucumber salad on the side is a good match.

Serves 4

for the eggplant
4 eggplant, halved
1 tablespoon Umami Paste (see page 15)
1½ teaspoons maple syrup
pinch of red pepper flakes or ground chile
1 teaspoon grated fresh ginger
3 scallions, thinly slice
3 tablespoons sesame seeds or Almond and Sesame Topping (see page 24)

for the cucumber salad
1 cucumber, sliced into ribbons
1 small shallot, finely sliced
2 tablespoons rice vinegar or raw apple cider vinegar
1 tablespoon maple syrup
1 teaspoon shoyu
sea salt and freshly ground black pepper

to serve
cooked grains or noodles

Preheat your broiler to the highest setting. Bring a large pan of water to a boil and set a steamer on top.

Cut a crosshatch pattern on the cut face of the eggplant halves, but not so deep that you pierce the skin. Put the eggplant halves in the steamer, cover, and cook for 6 to 8 minutes. Remove from the steamer and, if necessary, set aside on some paper towels to drain any excess moisture.

Meanwhile, make the cucumber salad. Combine all the salad ingredients in a bowl. Taste and adjust the seasoning if necessary. Set aside.

Mix the umami paste, 2½ tablespoons water, maple syrup, red pepper flakes, and ginger in a small bowl. Arrange the eggplant halves cut-side up on a baking sheet and brush the cut sides with the umami paste mixture. Broil for 3 to 5 minutes, until golden brown—keep an eye on them to make sure they don't burn.

Transfer the eggplant halves to a serving platter and sprinkle the scallions and sesame seeds or the topping over them. Serve with the cucumber salad and some cooked grains or noodles alongside.

SUSHI BOWLS WITH WASABI PEAS

Ask my daughter what she wants to eat, and one of the things she will shout out is, "A sushi bowl!" I couldn't agree more. I love to make sushi bowls—they're quick and easy and packed with flavor. When I prepare a meal with grains (quinoa or rice, for example), I always prepare more than I need, so I can make a sushi bowl the next day. It's not very complicated at all, and when you are pressed for time, this is an excellent idea for a healthy meal.

Serves 4

1¼ cups uncooked quinoa (or about 3 cups cooked)
10½ ounces frozen peas, thawed
2 to 3 teaspoons wasabi paste (or 2 teaspoons wasabi powder mixed with 1½ teaspoons water)
½ teaspoon salt, or more to taste
2 teaspoons sushi vinegar or brown rice vinegar
3 ripe avocados, halved and pitted
½ cucumber, finely sliced
handful of micro sprouts
2½ ounces Little Gem lettuce, leaves separated
¼ red cabbage, finely shredded
1 sheet of nori, snipped finely with scissors
Red Onion Pickle (see page 42) or ¼ cup finely chopped scallions
¼ cup Almond and Sesame Topping (see page 24) or toasted sesame seeds

for the dressing
¼ cup soy sauce
1 tablespoon sushi vinegar or brown rice vinegar
1 to 2 teaspoons grated fresh ginger (optional)

Cook the quinoa according to the package instructions (or use 3 cups leftover cooked quinoa or rice).

Combine the peas, wasabi paste, salt, vinegar, and the flesh of one avocado in a food processor and pulse until the mixture is combined but pieces of the peas are still visible—the texture doesn't have to be completely smooth. Taste and adjust the seasoning. Set aside.

Make the dressing. Combine all the dressing ingredients with 2 tablespoons water in a small bowl and set aside.

Peel and thinly slice the remaining 2 avocados.

Divide the quinoa among four bowls. Put 2 to 3 tablespoons of the wasabi peas in each bowl. Arrange the avocado and cucumber slices, sprouts, salad greens, shredded cabbage, nori, and pickled onion on top of the quinoa, making sure you don't mix the individual ingredients. Sprinkle with the topping or sesame seeds and pour the dressing over the bowls. *Oishii!*

CHICKPEA SHAWARMA AND CUCUMBER TZATZIKI

It's been a while since I last walked the streets after a night out in search for something to eat, but I am pretty sure that shawarma is still a favorite late-night snack (at least, it is in Holland). The dish originates from the Levantine kitchen and it's still a very popular street food on the Arabian peninsula and beyond. What makes this dish so attractive? To my mind, shawarma is all about the spices and the sauce. With this recipe, you can rustle up a quick and lovely shawarma, one so good that you'll want to run home to make it after a good night out rather than searching for a late-night food place.

Serves 4

for the shawarma spice mix
2 teaspoons ground cumin
2 teaspoons ground cinnamon
2 teaspoons sweet paprika
2 teaspoons freshly ground black pepper
1 teaspoon ground chile
½ teaspoon ground turmeric
2 teaspoons garlic powder
1 teaspoon ground allspice

for the chickpeas and tomatoes
2 tomatoes, chopped
2 (14½-ounce) cans chickpeas, drained and rinsed (or 3 cups drained cooked chickpeas)
salt
whole-grain pita breads, to serve

for the tzatziki
1 cucumber, seeded and grated
2 or 3 garlic cloves
1 teaspoon fresh lemon juice
scant ½ cup natural plant-based yogurt (or use Cashew Sour Cream; see page 17)
good pinch of salt
3 tablespoons chopped fresh dill or mint (optional)

Make the shawarma spice mix by simply combining all the spices together.

Make the chickpeas and tomatoes. Heat a dry pan. When it is hot, add the tomatoes and cook for 1 to 2 minutes, then add 1 to 1½ tablespoons of the shawarma spice mix (see Tip) and the chickpeas. Cook, stirring frequently and adding a splash of water if needed to prevent burning, until the chickpeas are hot, about 5 minutes.

Meanwhile, make the tzatziki. Combine all the tzatziki ingredients in a bowl and season to taste.

Serve the chickpea shawarma with whole-grain pita or cooked grains, topped with some tzatziki. You can also serve tahini sauce, some lettuce, pickles (see page 42), olives, and maybe some smoky paprika hummus (opposite) to make a real festive Middle Eastern meal.

> TIP:
> The shawarma spice mix here will make a bit more than you need. Just store it in a small container and you will be prepared for your next use. If you'd like, substitute 1 to 1½ tablespoons baharat spice mix in place of the shawarma spices.

HARISSA AND GRILLED PAPRIKA HUMMUS

If there is one prepared dish that is always in my fridge, it is hummus. I have jars of cooked chickpeas in my cellar, ready to make hummus and, of course, for the chickpea liquid (aquafaba) from the jar that I use as an egg substitute in many vegan dishes. I serve hummus on bread, as a dip for raw vegetables, as part of a mezze, as a sauce for whole roasted vegetables, or even stirred into a pasta dish. The possibilities are endless, which makes it a firm family favorite. This recipe makes quite a large amount and is intended to be eaten as a main dish. Hopefully, it will provide some leftovers for the following day, but I can't promise that.

Makes 4 cups

1½ teaspoons cumin seeds
2 (14½-ounce) cans chickpeas, drained
   and rinsed (or 3 cups drained cooked
   chickpeas; reserve 2 tablespoons for garnish)
2 roasted red peppers, homemade or
   store-bought (if store-bought, ensure that
   they are sugar-free)
2 generous tablespoons tahini
3 to 5 garlic cloves, chopped
1½ tablespoons harissa paste
salt

to serve
2 tablespoons sesame seeds (white, black, or
   a mix)
handful of fresh soft herbs, such as mint, dill, or
   cilantro
Flatbreads (see page 27) or pita bread
Pickles (see page 42)
raw vegetables, such as multicolored carrots
   and beets, cucumber, pepper, crispy salad
   greens, tomatoes, radishes, etc.

Toast the cumin seeds in a dry skillet until fragrant, a minute or less—stay near the pan and stir often to prevent burning. Transfer the seeds to a food processor or blender.

Add the chickpeas, roasted peppers, tahini, garlic, harissa paste, and ¾ cup water and blend until smooth. Taste and season with salt. Transfer the hummus to a large bowl.

To serve, top with the sesame seeds, fresh herbs, and the reserved whole chickpeas. Serve with the bread, pickles, and raw vegetables alongside.

OYSTER MUSHROOM BURGERS WITH GRILLED PAPRIKA MAYONNAISE

If there is one thing that's clear to me, it's that I am never going to eat a "real" burger again. And who needs one, anyway? Plant-based burgers are full of flavor, far more interesting, and so much better for you (and the environment) than meat-based ones. Of course, you can make a burger from beans and grains, but for a quick fix, I choose meaty oyster mushrooms on a bun.

Serves 4

1 pound oyster mushrooms
4 whole-grain buns, halved
salad greens
2 tomatoes, sliced
1 avocado, halved, pitted, and sliced
Pickled Red Onions (see page 42)
 or sliced red onion

for the grilled paprika mayonnaise
14 ounces silken tofu, or 2 cups Cashew Sour
 Cream (see page 17)

1 (10½-ounce) jar roasted red peppers, drained
 (ensure that they are sugar-free)
½ teaspoon fennel seeds
½ teaspoon smoked paprika
½ teaspoon salt (use kala namak, or Indian black
 salt, for a more egg-like taste)
1 tablespoon raw apple cider vinegar
1 tablespoon apricot jam (ensure that
 it is sugar-free)

Preheat a grill pan or heat a panini press according to the manufacturer's instructions. When the pan is very hot, add the mushrooms and cook, undisturbed, for 2 to 4 minutes. You might want to press down on the mushrooms with a spatula or even place a small heavy pan on top of the mushrooms (ensure the bottom is clean first), which helps them go all crispy. If you wish, place the buns on the pan, too, cut-side down, and cook until grill marks appear.

While the mushrooms are cooking, make the mayonnaise. Combine all the mayonnaise

ingredients in a blender and blend until smooth. Transfer the mayonnaise to a bowl.

When the mushrooms are cooked, assemble your burgers. Place some greens on the bottom half of each bun, then top with tomatoes, mushrooms, avocado slices, and onion. Spread some of the mayonnaise over the cut side of the bun top or drizzle it over the filling, then close the buns. Ready!

CUCUMBER SOUP

When it's warm outside, I often don't feel like making difficult foods and instead start to prepare light and fresh dishes, like cold soups. There are different chilled soups that have their origin in warmer climes—think of Spanish gazpacho, French vichyssoise, Russian borscht, and Korean *naengguk*. In this recipe, a main ingredient is cucumber, which is super hydrating for the body and, along with the melon, gives this soup its fresh and cooling effect. That is what I look for in the height of summer.

Serves 4 to 6 as a starter (makes 6 cups)

2 cucumbers, roughly chopped
3 scallions
1 small bunch fresh mint, chopped
1 small bunch fresh dill, chopped
2 garlic cloves, finely chopped
juice of 1 lemon
1 teaspoon salt
good pinch of ground chile
1 cup plant-based milk
1 avocado, pitted and peeled

toppings
¼ cantaloupe or honeydew melon, seeded
cucumber ribbons (sliced with a vegetable
  peeler)
1 teaspoon black sesame seeds or nigella seeds
1 teaspoon cracked pink peppercorns or red
  pepper flakes
dill sprigs

Start by scooping out some balls from your melon. Use a round melon baller or a small measuring spoon (a teaspoon is a good size). If you don't have this equipment, just cut your melon into ¾- to 1-inch cubes. Set the melon balls aside with the other soup toppings.

Make the soup. Combine all the soup ingredients in a blender and blend until smooth (you may need to do this in two batches if your blender is small). Taste and add a bit more salt or chile if needed. The soup should be refreshing, so don't go overboard on the chile. Divide the soup among four to six bowls and add the toppings to each individual bowl.

TIP:
This soup can easily be made in advance. Chill it in the fridge for a couple of hours before serving.

NINA'S LENTIL CHILI

Sometimes you eat such a delicious dish that the recipe becomes a part of your repertoire. This was the case with one from Nina Olsson's book *Bowls of Goodness*. The original name of her recipe is Loyal Lentil Chili. Since I first tried it, I have now cooked her lentil chili so many times while adjusting it here and there. I am sharing my version of her recipe here.

Serves 4

3 scallions, sliced into ½-inch pieces
4 garlic cloves, finely chopped
1 (1-inch) piece fresh ginger, grated
1 teaspoon ground cinnamon
1½ tablespoons garam masala
1 teaspoon cumin seeds
1 teaspoon smoked paprika
1 teaspoon ground turmeric
14 ounces chopped tomatoes (fresh or canned)
1½ cups drained cooked lentils (see page 32)
1⅔ cups coconut milk

2 medium sweet potatoes, peeled and coarsely
  grated
2 teaspoons Umami Paste (see page 15)
2 teaspoons hot sauce (try my sambal; see
  page 90)
1 tablespoon maple syrup
7 ounces greens, such as spinach or kale
salt or shoyu

Sweat the scallions with a splash of water in a large nonstick pan until softened, then add the garlic, ginger, cinnamon, garam masala, cumin, paprika, and turmeric. Cook, stirring and adding a splash of water if needed to avoid burning. When the onions are coated with the spices, add the tomatoes, lentils, coconut milk, sweet potato, umami paste, hot sauce, and maple syrup. Stir well, bring to a boil, then reduce the heat to maintain a simmer and cook for 10 minutes. Add the greens and cook for 1 to 2 minutes more, until they have wilted. Taste and add more salt, if needed, or use a dash of shoyu, then serve.

TIP:
Serve the chili with some cooked grains (like quinoa) or flatbreads, pickles (see page 42), and a dollop of Cashew Sour Cream (see page 17) or plant-based natural yogurt.

GREEK-INSPIRED BUTTER BEAN STEW

When I lived in Amsterdam, my husband and I often went out to dinner with my parents. One of my favorite place was a family-owned Greek restaurant. I really loved how their focus was always on good, fresh food. The Greek kitchen relies on fresh ingredients in dishes that are not complicated to make. Fresh herbs, such as oregano, mint, bay leaves, dill, parsley, basil, fennel seeds, and thyme, are a prominent feature. This recipe, which is based on the popular *gigandes plaki* (giant beans), makes use of these typical Greek herbs. They turn a simple weekday meal into a quick trip to Greece.

Serves 3 or 4

1 medium zucchini, quartered lengthwise
    and sliced
3 or 4 garlic cloves
2 teaspoons dried oregano, or 1½ tablespoons
    chopped fresh oregano
¾ teaspoon ground cinnamon
1 teaspoon fennel seeds
14 ounces chopped tomatoes, fresh or canned

1½ cups drained cooked butter beans (or one
    14-ounce can, drained and rinsed)
1 bay leaf
2 cups bulgur wheat
salt and freshly ground black pepper
2 tablespoons fresh dill or flat-leaf parsley,
    to serve

Combine the zucchini, garlic, and 2 to 3 tablespoons water in a pan and cook, stirring, over medium heat for 1 to 2 minutes. Stir in the oregano, cinnamon, and fennel seeds. Add the tomatoes, butter beans, and bay leaf and bring to a boil. Reduce the heat to medium-low and simmer for 8 to 12 minutes.

Meanwhile, cook the bulgur wheat according to the instructions on the package.

Once the stew and the bulgur wheat are cooked, taste them and add salt as needed. Scatter the fresh dill over the top and serve hot.

TIP:
For a more extensive meal, add tzatziki (see page 118), a tomato salad, and some Kalamata olives. You can also serve the stew with the vegan feta from my previous book, *Vegan in 7*.

NEW POTATO SALAD WITH RADISHES AND PEAS

Over the past few years, it has seemed that the potato has become less popular as a staple in comparison with more exotic options like rice or noodles. In Holland, the potato was once an essential everyday ingredient. Cooked potatoes were served almost every day, with another vegetable (like cauliflower) and a piece of meat, at precisely six o'clock. In my home, we mashed the two vegetables together on our plate and poured the gravy from the meat over the top. In the old days, if you were very poor, you ate only potatoes. Take a look at Vincent van Gogh's famous painting *The Potato Eaters*. Also, one of the most famous varieties of potatoes—Bintje—comes from the Netherlands. Nowadays, people no longer see the beauty of this ingredient, which is a shame. The potato is nourishing and gentle on the digestive system. The arrival of new potatoes always excites me, and the recipe for this salad is a beautiful example of how good a potato can be.

Serves 4 as a main, 6 as a starter

1 pound 10 ounces baby potatoes, halved (larger ones quartered)
9 ounces peas (thawed, if frozen)
1¼ cups natural plant-based yogurt or Cashew Sour Cream (see page 17)
2 teaspoons mustard, such as Dijon
1 tablespoon raw apple cider vinegar or fresh lemon juice

1 small bunch chives, finely chopped
1 small bunch flat-leaf parsley, finely chopped
1 or 2 garlic cloves, finely chopped (optional)
1 small bunch radishes, sliced
salt and freshly ground black pepper

Put the potatoes in a pan, cover with cold water, and bring to a boil. Cook the potatoes for 5 to 7 minutes, until they are cooked through but not overcooked and can be easily pierced with a sharp-pointed knife. In the last minute of cooking, add the peas. Drain the potatoes and peas in a colander and set aside.

Combine the yogurt, mustard, vinegar, chives, parsley, and garlic in a large bowl and add salt and pepper to taste. Tip in the potatoes, peas, and radishes. Gently stir to combine everything until all the potatoes are covered with sauce. Mix gently—you don't want to break up the potatoes too much. Serve immediately or cover and refrigerate until ready to serve.

TIP:
This salad is good served with pickled onions (see page 42) on the side.

GREEN PUDDING FOR ONE

During the year, I usually go through different phases of what I like for breakfast. In the winter it is generally porridge, then, when I have had enough, I switch to granola. When spring comes, and then finally summer, I crave fresh fruits. This pudding is an example of what I eat regularly once the weather improves and the sun begins to shine.

Serves 1

2 medium bananas, peeled and cut into chunks
1 avocado, halved, pitted, and peeled
zest and juice of 1 organic lime
2 tablespoons maple syrup, plus more if needed
handful of spinach, washed

for the toppings
1 green apple, quartered, cored, and sliced
1 kiwi fruit, peeled and sliced
blueberries or blackberries

Combine the bananas, avocado, lime zest, lime juice, maple syrup, and spinach in a blender and blend until smooth. Taste and add more sweetener, if desired. Pour the mixture into a pretty bowl, add the toppings, and devour.

TIP:
It's easy to make this simple pudding to serve more than one—just multiply the ingredients by the number of people. If you freeze this pudding, it turns into a delicious "ice cream."

SWEET CELEBRATIONS

Celebrations are often associated with sweets.
For a birthday or a wedding you eat cake or tart;
for other festive events in the calendar, such
as Christmas or Easter, you may have a nice
dessert. For less special occasions we still enjoy
something sweet: a cookie with our tea, or a
muffin or cinnamon bun for a quick snack. Most
of the treats you can buy are overly processed
and unhealthy, and contain lots of sugar, milk,
and butter. So I make my own vegan ones that do
not contain any refined sugars, milk, or butter.
As I explained in the introduction, a high-speed
blender is a great tool for making super-smooth
vegan creams. This chapter includes a super-
light chocolate mousse and various cakes, tarts,
cookies, and muffins that are delicious and
healthy at the same time, so you can indulge in a
sweet treat on regular or special occasions.

AQUAFABA CHOCOLATE MOUSSE

There has been a lot of talk about aquafaba recently. It may sound like an exotic ingredient, but in fact, aquafaba is just the more appealing word for the thick liquid that forms from cooking certain pulses, such as white beans and chickpeas. Aquafaba (coined from the Latin words for "water" and "bean") is usually rinsed off and discarded. However, it is a precious ingredient for the vegan cook, because it can be used as an egg substitute for baking, giving dishes an airy and eggy texture. When whipped up, aquafaba develops a meringue-like consistency. My light-as-air chocolate mousse is a perfect example of how good this egg substitute is (3 tablespoons aquafaba equals 1 egg).

Serves 4

scant ½ cup aquafaba, chilled
2 tablespoons maple syrup
4 ounces vegan chocolate, preferably 70% cacao and sweetened with coconut sugar, roughly

chopped
½ teaspoon vanilla powder
pinch of salt

Pour the aquafaba into the bowl of a stand mixer fitted with the whisk attachment (or into a large bowl, if using a handheld mixer) and beat for 4 to 6 minutes, until stiff white peaks form. Add the maple syrup to the mixture and gently fold it in using a metal spoon.

Put the chocolate in a separate heatproof bowl and place it over a pan of simmering water, ensuring that the water is not in contact with the bottom of the bowl. Add the vanilla powder and salt to the chocolate and stir to combine. When the chocolate has melted, remove the bowl from the heat and let cool for a minute.

Gently fold the cooled chocolate mixture into the whipped aquafaba using a spatula. Divide the chocolate mousse among four small bowls or glasses and refrigerate for at least 1 hour to set.

You can serve the mousse as it is or top it with berries, a dusting of ground cinnamon, cacao nibs, or even a small amount of red pepper flakes.

FROZEN BANANA ICE POPS

At the height of summer when the weather is too hot for anything, a refreshing ice pop comes to the rescue, so you run to the store to get one. But for me, even the ones "labeled" vegan are not very appealing. Store-bought ice pops are full of sugars, such as corn syrup, refined sugar, or sugar syrup, so I prefer to make my own using bananas and nuts. **You will need 12 wooden ice pop sticks.**

Makes 12

6 ripe but firm medium bananas
1 jar or package creamed coconut
  or coconut butter (at least 7 ounces), sealed
  in its original packaging
1⅔ cups raw cashews, soaked overnight and
  drained
¾ cup nut milk

½ teaspoon vanilla powder
5 tablespoons maple syrup
pinch of salt
2 ounces blueberries (thawed, if frozen; I prefer
  wild blueberries, if you can get them)
2½ tablespoons cacao or carob powder

Line a baking sheet with parchment paper. Peel the bananas, then halve them crosswise. Gently insert a wooden stick vertically into the center of each piece so it runs about halfway through the banana. Lay them on the lined baking sheet and freeze for 2 to 3 hours, until firm.

Meanwhile, bring some water to a simmer in a small pan. Place the creamed coconut or coconut butter, still in its packaging, in the water and heat until it becomes liquid. If the package size was more than 7 ounces, measure 7 ounces into a high-speed blender and reserve the rest for another use.

Add the soaked cashews, nut milk, vanilla powder, maple syrup, and salt to the blender and blend until the mixture is very smooth. Pour half the mixture into a bowl and set aside. Add the thawed blueberries to the remaining mixture

in the blender and blend well. Pour the blueberry mixture into a glass.

Return the mixture without blueberries back to the blender, add the cacao powder, and blend until well combined. Pour this into a second glass.

Take the frozen bananas out of the freezer and dip six of them into the blueberry-cashew mixture, gently shaking off any excess and making sure each one is coated before placing it back on the lined baking sheet. Dip the remaining six bananas into the chocolate-cashew mixture in the same manner. Return the bananas to the freezer for at least 3 hours to set the coating. Enjoy them straight from the freezer.

CRÈME BRÛLÉE AUX MARRONS

You may think chestnuts are a typical Christmas ingredient, but for me they are not. The official hunt for chestnuts in our family begins in Holland, in the first or second week of October. However, the most beautiful and tastiest ones grow in France, in the Ardèche region, where they are protected as carefully as French wine. Chestnuts from the Ardèche have their own *Appellation d'Origine Protégée* (AOP), a certification of their quality and source. The French are rightly proud of their regional produce, and Ardèche chestnuts are used in a variety of products. One of them is *crème de marrons*, a sweet chestnut paste made with vanilla and sugar. It has a beautiful caramel-like taste and is often eaten on pancakes or added to cakes and tarts. In this recipe I combine my own *crème de marrons* with another famous French dessert: crème brûlée.

Serves 4 to 6

¾ cup raw cashews, soaked overnight and drained

10½ ounces unsweetened cooked chestnuts, crumbled

1 teaspoon vanilla powder

6 tablespoons maple syrup

scant 1 cup plant-based milk (I use almond milk)

pinch of salt

scant ½ cup aquafaba (see page 135), chilled for at least 3 hours

4 to 6 tablespoons coconut sugar

Combine the cashews, crumbled chestnuts, vanilla, maple syrup, milk, and salt in a high-speed blender and blend until very smooth. You might want to use the tamper and push down the mass from time to time to get a really soft, creamy result. Set aside.

Pour the aquafaba into the bowl of a stand mixer fitted with the whisk attachment (or into a large bowl, if using a handheld mixer) and beat for 4 to 6 minutes, until stiff white peaks form. Add the chestnut paste and beat briefly until combined. Scoop the chestnut mousse into four or six ovenproof ramekins. Refrigerate the mousse for 1 to 2 hours to firm up.

Preheat the broiler to high. Spoon 1 tablespoon of the coconut sugar over each chestnut mousse. Shake the ramekins back and forth to ensure the sugar is in an even layer and set them on a rimmed baking sheet. Slide the baking sheet under the broiler and cook for about 5 minutes to caramelize the sugar, rotating the ramekins frequently to make sure the topping cooks evenly; keep your eye on them—you don't want the coconut sugar to burn. Remove the ramekins and let cool a little. You can either serve them warm or put them back in the fridge to serve chilled—but note that if you leave them in the fridge for too long, the topping may turn into caramel.

TIPS:
Add 3 tablespoons cacao or carob powder to the chestnut mousse to make a *crème de marrons et du chocolat*.

Alternatively, skip the coconut sugar layer and serve this as a chilled mousse topped with some seasonal fruits, such as pomegranate seeds, clementine segments, or cape gooseberries.

OVEN-ROASTED FIGS, GRAPES, AND PEARS WITH ICE CREAM

In the summer, we all want to eat more raw fruits, crisp vegetables, and fresh salads, and use cooking methods that are not overly complicated to keep the produce light and fresh. Come autumn, my focus is on bringing gentle heat to my dishes. This means using warming spices, such as cinnamon, and turning on the oven, even for fruit desserts. Baked fruit becomes sweeter and softer, and the flavor is changed and intensified—as this simple recipe shows.

Serves 4 to 6

4 ripe but firm pears, peeled
8 figs, quartered
9 ounces red grapes
9 ounces blackberries (thawed, if frozen)
1 bay leaf
1 cinnamon stick
6 tablespoons apple, grape, or orange juice

for the ice cream
5 ripe bananas, sliced, then frozen for at least 6 hours
1 teaspoon vanilla powder
¼ cup plant-based milk (coconut is good)
a few drops of liquid stevia (optional)

Preheat the oven to 400°F. Quarter and core the pears, then slice each quarter into halves or thirds (the pieces should be roughly the same size as the quartered figs). Put all the fruits into a shallow baking dish with the bay leaf, cinnamon, and fruit juice. Bake for 20 to 25 minutes, until the fruits have become sticky and the juices start to bubble. Remove the dish from the oven and set aside while you make the ice cream.

Combine the frozen bananas, vanilla, milk, and stevia (if using) in a high-speed blender and blend until smooth, using the tamper to push the bananas down and facilitate blending. (You will have to use a high-speed blender, or you risk damaging the motor of an ordinary blender. You can also use a food processor; just be sure to stop to scrape down the sides from time to time.) The bananas will be grainy at first, but keep going and the texture will become softer. Keep an eye on the texture—you want it to reach a soft-serve consistency but not become soupy or too liquid.

Pour the mixture into a container and freeze for 30 minutes. Serve with the roasted fruits.

TIPS:
Use ripe, spotted bananas for the ice cream, because they will be sweetest. You can also make the ice cream in advance and freeze it until needed. Any leftovers can be served the following day on porridge or pancakes.

When you don't feel like making ice cream, serve the roasted fruits with coconut yogurt or Cashew Sour Cream (see page 17).

GRILLED PEACHES WITH GINGER CREAM AND WALNUT PRALINE

The perfectly ripe peach is a tricky thing to find. Most peaches are too hard when you buy them, and if you take them home to ripen, it is difficult to keep track of when they are soft, scented, and sweet. Not to discourage you—no, not at all! For this recipe, you can use peaches that are not perfectly ripe. You'll need a stovetop grill pan or a panini press.

Serves 4

1½ cups Cashew Sour Cream (see page 17)
  or coconut yogurt
2 teaspoons grated fresh ginger
1½ teaspoons ground cinnamon
½ teaspoon freshly grated nutmeg (optional)
½ teaspoon vanilla powder
pinch of salt

¼ cup maple or brown rice syrup
6 ripe but firm peaches, halved and pitted

for the praline
1 cup walnuts
2 tablespoons maple syrup
pinch of salt

Combine the cashew sour cream, ginger, cinnamon, nutmeg (if using), vanilla, and salt in a bowl. Set aside. (You can do this in advance; cover and refrigerate until ready to use.)

Toast the walnuts in a dry nonstick or cast-iron pan over medium heat, stirring frequently, for 3 to 4 minutes, until golden brown. Add the maple syrup and salt and stir to coat. Cook for a minute more, then tip the walnuts out of the pan and spread them on a sheet of parchment paper. Once the walnuts are cool, roughly chop them.

Heat a grill pan over high heat or preheat a panini press according to the manufacturer's instructions. The pan must be really hot before you start to grill the peaches. Lay the fruit cut-side down on the pan and cook for 3 minutes, or until grill marks appear. Serve with sour cream, maple syrup, and walnut praline.

TIP:
For a festive flourish, use some fresh lemon verbena or mint leaves or dried lavender flowers (make sure they're culinary-grade) as an extra topping.

BANANA AND TOFFEE PARFAIT

"Cake in a glass" is the only way to describe this delightful parfait. It is based on the very popular banana-and-toffee pie known as "banoffee pie." Traditionally, it is made with a sugar-based caramel and dairy cream, but in this recipe, I use Medjool dates for the caramel and cashew cream as a dairy substitute. What's not to love about this healthy take on a classic?

Serves 4

for the crust
5¼ ounces Medjool dates (about 8), pitted
1 cup raw walnuts
2 tablespoons carob or cacao powder
pinch of salt

for the date caramel
5¼ ounces Medjool dates (about 8), pitted
5 tablespoons peanut butter (almond butter or tahini also work)
¼ teaspoon vanilla powder
good pinch of salt

for the cream
1¼ cups Cashew Sour Cream (see page 17) or coconut yogurt
2 tablespoons maple syrup or brown rice syrup
¼ teaspoon vanilla powder

to assemble
3 ripe but firm bananas, peeled and sliced

Make the crumb layer. Combine all the crumb layer ingredients in a food processor and process until the mixture resembles coarse crumbs. Set aside.

Make the date caramel. Combine the dates, peanut butter, vanilla, salt, and ¾ cup water in a blender. Blend until smooth, adding a splash more water if the texture is a bit too dense. Transfer the caramel to a bowl and set aside.

Make the cream. Combine the cashew sour cream, maple syrup, and vanilla in a medium bowl and stir until well combined.

To assemble the parfaits, spoon 2 to 3 tablespoons of the crumb layer into the bottom of each of four glasses. Add 2 to 3 tablespoons of the caramel to each, then a couple of banana slices, and finally top with a layer of the cream. Repeat the layers if any ingredients remain and you have space in your glass, or finish by adding a couple of sliced bananas on top of your cream layer.

Serve immediately, or make ahead and refrigerate until ready to serve.

RASPBERRY AND COCONUT CHEESECAKE

This cheesecake has been a part of my repertoire for many, many years. It's an easy recipe, and once you have made it a couple of times, I am sure it will be one of your favorites, too. Here I use raspberries, but all kinds of berries work well in this recipe, as do other fruits, such as mango, kiwi, persimmon, and pineapple. I have tried all these, and they are equally delicious.

Serves 12

for the crust
1⅓ cups almond flour
100g fine oat flakes
3 tablespoons nut butter
3 to 4 tablespoons maple or brown rice syrup
pinch of salt

for the filling
4 cups coconut milk
1 teaspoon vanilla powder
scant ½ cup maple syrup

juice of ½ lemon
1 tablespoon nutritional yeast (optional)
1 tablespoon agar agar
3 tablespoons cornstarch or arrowroot powder, combined with 3 tablespoons water

for the raspberry topping
1 pound raspberries (thawed, if frozen)
¾ cup apple juice
3 tablespoons cornstarch or arrowroot powder, combined with 3 tablespoons water

---

Make the crust. Preheat the oven to 350°F and line a 9-inch cake pan with a removable bottom with parchment paper.

Combine all the crust ingredients in a large bowl and mix with a fork to create a crumbly texture. With moist hands, form the mixture into a ball and transfer to the lined pan. Firmly press it into an even layer over the bottom of the pan. Bake for 12 to 15 minutes until the crust is lightly golden. Remove the pan from the oven and set the crust aside to cool while you make the filling.

Make the filling. Combine the coconut milk, vanilla, maple syrup, lemon juice, nutritional yeast (if using), and agar agar in a pan. Bring to a gentle boil over medium-low heat, stirring continuously with a whisk. It is important to keep whisking at this stage, or the agar agar will form clumps, which you want to avoid. Cook, stirring,

for about 6 minutes. Add the arrowroot mixture and stir until the filling thickens, about 1 minute (this happens quickly, so keep an eye on the pan). Pour the filling over the cooled crust. Let the filling cool for 2 to 3 hours to become firm. (Once the initial heat has gone, you can transfer the cake to the fridge to cool further.)

When the filling has firmed up completely, make the raspberry topping. Put the raspberries in a bowl and set aside. Pour the apple juice into a small pan and bring to a low boil. Stir the cornstarch mixture, then, while whisking, add it to the apple juice and continue to whisk briskly until the mixture thickens. Pour the mixture over the raspberries and gently stir to coat.

Carefully pour the topping over the filling. Let it cool completely to set. Serve, or store in an airtight container in the fridge for up to 2 days.

APRICOT CLAFOUTIS

Clafoutis is a French baked dessert, like a flan made with batter and cherries. You can make it with other stone fruits such as plums, peaches or apricots, although purists will tell you that if you use anything other than cherries, it isn't a clafoutis and should be called a *flaugnarde instead*. In this recipe I have used apricots, and the batter is a vegan version instead of the traditional milk, eggs, and flour one, but I'm sticking with the name "clafoutis." The recipe is not complicated at all and it can be eaten warm or chilled and, if you like, served with some Cashew Sour Cream (see page 17) or coconut yogurt.

Serves 6

1 pound ripe but firm apricots, halved and pitted

¼ cup plus 2 teaspoons cornstarch

1¼ cups plus 2 tablespoons almond milk
  (or other plant-based milk)

scant ¾ cup almond flour

3 tablespoons sugar-free applesauce

5 tablespoons maple syrup or brown rice syrup

½ teaspoon vanilla powder

Preheat the oven to 400°F. Arrange the apricots cut-side up in a ceramic baking dish.

In a large bowl, mix the cornstarch with 3 tablespoons of the almond milk until dissolved. Add the rest of the almond milk, the almond flour, applesauce, maple syrup, and vanilla and mix until no lumps remain, then pour the batter over the apricots in the baking dish.

Bake for about 35 minutes, or until the batter is bubbling, golden, and set in the center. Remove from the oven and let cool for at least 30 minutes before serving.

RAW MANGO MOUSSE MINI CAKES

For a long time, I was on a raw food diet. During that period, everything I ate had to be raw, which means nothing heated above 108°F. The idea is that if food isn't cooked or otherwise brought to high temperatures, the micronutrients in the food stay alive and can contribute to better health when eaten. With this diet came new ideas and innovative techniques for making cakes, mousses, and creams with nuts. Although I no longer eat a raw food diet full-time, I still use these techniques. These delicious mini cakes are one example.

Makes 12

for the crust
¾ cup unsweetened desiccated coconut
½ cup almonds
8 Medjool dates, pitted

for the filling
1 jar or package creamed coconut (at least
  7 ounces), sealed in its original packaging
5¼ ounces dried mango, soaked overnight
1⅔ cups raw cashews, soaked overnight

½ teaspoon vanilla powder
juice of 2 limes
¾ cup plus 2 tablespoons coconut milk
6 tablespoons maple syrup or brown rice syrup
½ teaspoon ground turmeric (optional, for color)
small pinch of salt

for the topping
2 fresh mangoes, thinly sliced

Line each well of a 12-cup muffin tin with two long perpendicular strips of parchment paper (this will help you remove the cakes pan once they are frozen). The paper needs to stick to the base and sides a little so that it is easy to lift out the cakes. (If you are using a silicone muffin pan, there's no need to line it with parchment.)

Make the crust. Combine the desiccated coconut, almonds, and dates in a food processor and process until finely chopped and the mixture holds together when pressed. Place 1½ tablespoons into each cup of the prepared tin. Firmly press the crust into the cup using your fingers or the bottom of a small glass. Set aside.

Make the filling. Bring a small saucepan of water to a simmer. Place the creamed coconut, still in its packaging, in the water and heat until it

becomes liquid. If the package was more than 7 ounces, measure 7 ounces into a high-speed blender and reserve the rest for another use.

Drain the soaked mango and cashew and add them to the blender. Add the vanilla, lime juice, ¾ cup of the coconut milk, the maple syrup, turmeric (if using), and salt. Blend until very smooth, adding a bit more coconut milk, a few tablespoons at a time, if needed to keep the machine going. Pour 3½ to 4 tablespoons into each muffin cup. Freeze for 2 to 3 hours.

Remove the pan from the freezer 30 minutes before you wish to serve. Decorate the mini cakes with the fresh mango and serve immediately. These mini cakes are a bit like ice cream; they won't hold their shape too long once they are out of the fridge or freezer.

TIP:
These mini cakes can easily be made in advance and frozen. Take them out of the freezer 30 minutes before serving and decorate them with the fresh mango just before eating.

OATMEAL AND RAISIN COOKIES

Not a fan of oatmeal? You should be! Oatmeal is high in fiber and protein and a source of important vitamins, minerals, and antioxidants. Many studies have proven the health benefits of eating oats, including lower blood sugar levels, weight loss, and reduced chance of constipation. Oats are often eaten in the morning as oatmeal, but it is also a wonderful grain to give texture and bite to baked goods and cookies. This recipe is quick and simple—perfect when you have unexpected visitors for tea or when you fancy a cookie for breakfast instead of a bowl of oatmeal.

Makes 8 to 10

1 cup plus 2 tablespoons whole-grain spelt flour
½ cup rolled oats
scant ½ cup maple syrup
scant ½ cup peanut butter (or other nut butter)

½ cup raisins
¼ teaspoon vanilla powder
pinch of salt

Preheat the oven to 350°F and line a baking sheet with parchment paper.

Mix all the ingredients in a bowl until combined and knead to make a dough. If any raisins drop out of the mixture, just push them back in.

I like to use measuring cups (¼ cup or ⅓ cup, depending on how large I want my cookies) to get my cookies more or less the same size. Push some of the dough into the measuring cup and take it out to form a ball. Set the ball on the lined baking sheet and flatten it with a spatula or the bottom of the measuring cup. Some cracks may

appear in the rim of the cookie—if you wish, you can seal them with the palms of your (slightly moist) hands. The cookies don't have to look overly pretty, though—they are meant to be a bit rustic. Repeat until all the dough has been used.

Bake the cookies for 15 to 17 minutes, until golden brown. Remove from the oven and let cool on the baking sheet for 10 minutes before transferring to a wire rack to cool completely. To keep them crunchy, store the cookies in a jar with a tight-fitting lid. They will keep at room temperature for 4 to 5 days.

APRICOT, CARDAMOM, AND PISTACHIO BISCOTTI

There are many different cookies—soft and chewy, crisp and thin, filled and dipped—and almost all of them go well with a cup of tea. A cup of tea is not only an English tradition, but a Dutch one, too. In Holland, the first tea and cookie of the day appear at about 10 a.m., and as a child, my mum would make me a cup of tea after school and serve a cookie with it. Perhaps in thousands, maybe millions, of other homes and cultures, it is the same. My favorite cookies are the ones like Italian biscotti or cantucci, which, being twice-baked, are crunchy and dry—perfect for dipping into a coffee or a glass of vin santo. However, I prefer them dipped in a cup of tea. These crisp, Italian-style biscotti are intended for just that.

Makes about 30 biscotti

6 tablespoons chilled aquafaba (see page 135)
scant 2 cups whole-grain spelt flour
1½ teaspoons ground cardamom
½ teaspoon vanilla powder
1 teaspoon baking powder

¾ cup coconut sugar
4½ tablespoons natural plant-based yogurt
¾ cup raw pistachios, roughly chopped
¾ cup unsulfured dried apricots, chopped into small chunks

Preheat the oven to 325°F and line a baking sheet with parchment paper.

Pour the aquafaba into the bowl of a stand mixer fitted with a whisk attachment (or a large bowl, if using a handheld mixer) and beat for 4 to 6 minutes, until stiff peaks form. Sift the flour into another bowl with the cardamom, vanilla, baking powder, and coconut sugar. Add the whipped aquafaba and the yogurt and gently mix. Add the pistachios and apricots and mix again.

Divide the dough in half. With slightly moist hands, form each half into a log about 12 inches long and 2 inches wide. Carefully transfer each log to the lined baking sheet and bake for 30 minutes in the middle of the oven.

Remove the pan from the oven and let the logs cool for 5 to 7 minutes (keep the oven on). Cut the logs crosswise into ½- to ¾-inch-thick slices—you will end up with about 30 slices. Lay the slices on the baking sheet and bake for 14 to 16 minutes more. Remove from the oven and transfer to a wire rack to cool completely, at least 1 hour, so they become really crunchy. They will keep in an airtight container at room temperature for at least 1 week.

TIP:
These cookies are meant to be dipped into hot herbal tea or a golden milk (see page 170).

BANANA MUFFINS WITH CRUMBLE TOPPING

Sometimes I keep bananas until their skins turn brown and spotty to increase their sweetness. Then I peel the bananas and freeze them for later use in ice cream, banana bread or these spicy muffins with their delicious crunchy topping. Because bananas have natural sweetness, you don't need a lot of additional sweetener. And did you know that one mashed banana can replace one egg in every baked goods recipe? So that is why I am "going bananas" over spotty brown bananas!

Makes 9

for the crumble topping
2 tablespoons fine oat flakes
1 tablespoon coconut sugar
1 tablespoon almond butter
¼ teaspoon ground cinnamon
pinch of salt

for the batter
2⅓ cups whole-grain spelt flour
1 teaspoon baking soda

1 teaspoon baking powder
1 teaspoon ground cinnamon
½ teaspoon ground ginger (optional)
¼ teaspoon vanilla powder
pinch of salt
3 ripe bananas, mashed
¾ cup natural plant-based yogurt
scant ½ cup maple syrup
½ cup walnuts, roughly chopped

Preheat the oven to 350°F and line 9 wells of a muffin tin with paper liners.

Make the crumble topping. Mix all the ingredients with a fork until they form a crumbly texture. Set aside.

Make the muffins. Combine the flour, baking soda, baking powder, cinnamon, ginger, vanilla, and salt in a large bowl. Add the mashed bananas, yogurt, and maple syrup to the dry ingredients. Gently mix with a spatula or whisk until combined. Add the walnuts and gently fold them into the batter.

Portion the batter into the prepared muffin cups, using an ice cream scoop or a measuring cup to keep the muffins the same size. Top each one with 1 teaspoon of the crumble topping. Bake the muffins for 20 to 24 minutes, until a wooden skewer inserted into the center of a muffin comes out clean; if there are some crumbs or moist dough clinging to it, cook them for a few minutes longer. Remove the pan from the oven and let the muffins cool. Store in an airtight container at room temperature for 4 to 5 days.

PLUM GALETTE

During a good plum year, I eat and make lots of plum dishes. In the area where we live in France, there are just so many varieties. First the purple Madeleine will be ripe, then the small yellow Mirabelle, then, in late August, the Quetsche, or damson plum. If there are plenty, it means I have buckets full. They will be eaten as a snack or in a tart. Some women in the village will preserve them in glass jars, to make plum cakes all year round. I prefer freezing them or, even better, eating them right away in an easy galette like this one.

Serves 6 to 8

for the dough
1⅓ cups whole-grain spelt flour
6 tablespoons almond butter
pinch of salt
1½ tablespoons coconut blossom sugar or maple syrup
6 to 7 tablespoons ice-cold water

for the filling
1 pound plums, halved, pitted and sliced
2 to 3 tablespoons coconut blossom sugar or maple syrup

¼ teaspoon vanilla powder
a few turns of black pepper (optional, but really good)
1 teaspoon cornstarch, arrowroot powder, or tapioca flour

for the glaze (optional)
2 tablespoons almond milk or other plant-based milk
1 tablespoon maple syrup
2 to 3 tablespoons coconut blossom sugar

Make the dough. Combine all the ingredients for the dough except the water in a food processor. Pulse, adding the cold water 1 tablespoon at a time, until the dough comes together. When all the water has been incorporated, the dough should still be a bit crumbly should hold together when pressed. Tip the dough out of the bowl and form it into a ball. Wrap the dough in plastic wrap and refrigerate for about 30 minutes (or put into the freezer for 10 minutes, if you are in a hurry).

Preheat the oven to 350°F and line a baking sheet with parchment paper.

Make the filling. Gently stir together the plums, sugar,, vanilla, pepper (if using), and cornstarch in a bowl. Set aside.

Remove the dough from the fridge and roll it out on a clean, lightly floured surface with a lightly floured rolling pin. (If it is hard to roll, let it sit for a few minutes at room temperature to soften slightly.) Form the dough into a round 12 to 15 inches in diameter and ¼ inch thick. Transfer the dough round to the lined baking sheet. Place the plum mixture in the center of the dough or fan it out to make the filling look prettier, leaving a 1½- to 2-inch border. Fold the border over the filling. Whisk the almond milk and maple syrup in a small bowl and brush it over the dough border, then sprinkle with the coconut blossom sugar.

Bake for 40 to 50 minutes, until the pastry is golden brown and the plums are cooked. Let cool. Serve as is or topped with a dollop of Cashew Sour Cream (see page 17) or coconut yogurt.

ORANGE AND ROSEMARY TARTLETS

Serving individual cakes must be the fanciest thing around and when I make them I almost feel like a real French pâtissier. If you don't usually have the patience to bake individual cakes, these tartlets are easy to make. Try to use blood oranges for the filling, they are so pretty and taste sweeter than regular oranges. You will need six individual tart tins, preferably ones with removable bases.

Makes 6

for the crust
2 tablespoons ground golden
  flaxseed
1 cup plus 1 tablespoon oat flour,
  plus extra for dusting
1 cup plus 1½ tablespoons almond flour
3 tablespoons maple syrup
3 tablespoons nut butter (white almond
  or cashew butter, if you want to keep
  the tartlets pale)
pinch of salt

for the cream filling
1⅓ cups raw cashews, soaked for at least
  30 minutes
1½ teaspoons orange zest
¾ cup fresh orange juice
½ teaspoon vanilla powder
1 teaspoon grated fresh ginger (optional)
2 to 3 tablespoons maple or brown rice syrup

to decorate
3 blood oranges, peeled and segmented
1 teaspoon finely chopped fresh rosemary leaves

Make the crust. Combine the ground flaxseeds with 6 tablespoons water in a small bowl and stir well. Set aside to thicken; this will be your flaxseed "egg."

In a large bowl, use a fork to combine the oat flour, almond flour, maple syrup, nut butter, flaxseed "egg," and salt until the mixture comes together into a dough. Form the dough into a ball and return it to the bowl. Cover the bowl with a plate and refrigerate for 20 to 30 minutes.

Preheat the oven to 350°F.

Make the filling. Combine all the filling ingredients in a high-speed blender and blend until very smooth. Transfer the filling to a container, cover, and refrigerate.

Remove the dough from the fridge and roll it out thinly, using a little more oat flour if it is sticking to your work surface. Use a cutter to stamp out rounds about 1 inch bigger than your tart tins. Drape the dough into six mini tart tins with removable bottoms, gently pushing it into the bottom and up the sides, and cut off any excess dough. Bake for 20 to 25 minutes, until golden brown. Remove from the oven and let cool enough to handle. Gently remove the crusts from the tins.

Distribute the orange cream filling among the crusts and decorate the tartlets with orange segments and a small sprinkle of finely chopped fresh rosemary. Serve immediately or refrigerate until ready to serve.

STRAWBERRY AND VANILLA CUSTARD TART

I think it's good to wait for the local strawberry season. Sure, we can get strawberries, and almost any other fruit, all year round, but it just isn't the same. The global market has meant we've lost touch with seasonality over the last few decades. In an age when everything seems possible, sometimes it is better to step back and start thinking about how things were done in the old days. Eagerly awaiting the season for a certain fruit or vegetable is one example. So when local strawberries are available, this recipe is highly recommended.

Serves 6 to 8

for the crust
1¾ cups almond flour
3 tablespoons arrowroot powder or cornstarch
¼ cup coconut sugar
5 tablespoons natural plant-based yogurt
pinch of salt

for the custard
1¾ cups almond milk (for a homemade version, see page 98)

¾ teaspoon vanilla powder
pinch of salt
4 to 5 tablespoons maple syrup or brown rice syrup
pinch of ground turmeric (optional, for color)
1 teaspoon agar agar
3 tablespoons cornstarch or arrowroot powder
1 pound 10 ounces strawberries, halved

Preheat the oven to 350°F and line an 8-inch removable bottom tart tin with parchment paper.

Make the crust. Combine all the ingredients for the crust in a large bowl and mix with a fork until a dough forms. Using slightly moist hands or the back of a spoon, press the dough over the bottom and up the sides of the lined tart tin, ensuring it is evenly distributed. (The dough is quite soft, so you might have to wet your hands again from time to time.)

Bake for 20 to 30 minutes, until golden brown. Remove the crust from the oven and let cool until cool enough to handle, then gently remove the crust from the tin.

Meanwhile, make the custard. Put the almond milk in a smal pan and bring to a gentle boil, then

add the vanilla, salt, 4 tablespoons of the maple syrup, the turmeric (if using), and the agar agar and cook, stirring continuously with a whisk, until the agar agar dissolves and there are no small lumps. Cook, whisking frequently, for 6 minutes more. Taste to check that it is sweet enough to your liking and add the remaining 1 tablespoon maple syrup, if needed.

Combine the cornstarch with 2 tablespoons water and add this to the custard. Cook, whisking briskly, until the custard has thickened, about 1 minute. Remove the custard from the heat and let it cool a little.

Pour the custard into the cooled tart crust. Let cool and set completely (you can transfer the tart to the fridge to speed up the process). When set, top the custard with the strawberries and serve.

RAW BROWNIE PETITS FOURS

When friends come over or I am invited somewhere for a meal, one of the things I often make is a treat that contains no refined sugar. A lot of people have their own ideas about being vegan and sugar-free, most of which are not very positive. But if they taste one of my sugar-free vegan treats, they are swept off their feet and ask me all sorts of questions. What did I use? How come they've never had this before? Is it really healthy? These pretty brownies will certainly impress your guests.

Makes about 30 pieces

for the base
10½ ounces Medjool dates, pitted
1½ cups unsweetened desiccated coconut
1½ cups raw walnuts
pinch of salt
½ teaspoon vanilla powder
¼ cup cacao or carob powder

for the cream layer
1 jar or packaged creamed coconut or
   coconut butter (at least 3½ ounces),
   sealed in its original packaging

1⅔ cups raw cashews, soaked overnight and
   drained
½ teaspoon vanilla powder
5 tablespoons maple syrup or brown rice syrup
½ cup plus 3 tablespoons coconut or almond
   milk, plus more if needed

topping suggestions
freeze-dried raspberries or strawberries, fresh
   berries or fruits, sesame seeds, chopped raw
   pistachios or cacao nibs, orange or lemon zest,
   and/or edible flowers

Line the bottom of a brownie pan with parchment paper (or use silicone ice cube trays, which do not need to be lined).

Make the base. Combine all the ingredients for the base in a food processor and pulse until evenly combined, scraping down the sides from time to time.

Press the mixture into the lined brownie pan (or into the ice cube trays, in which case leave some space in each for the second layer).

Make the cream layer. Bring some water to a simmer in a small pan. Place the creamed coconut, still in its packaging, in the water and heat until it becomes liquid. Measure 6 tablespoons into a high-speed blender and reserve the rest for another use.

Add the cashews, vanilla, maple syrup, 1¼ cups of the nut milk, and a pinch of salt. Blend until very smooth, stopping and scraping down the sides if needed and adding up to 4 teaspoons additional nut milk to ensure the mixture continues to blend. Spread the batter over the base layer in the pan or divide it among the ice cube wells. Refrigerate for at least 30 minutes.

When chilled, turn the brownie out of tin onto a cutting board and cut it into 30 petits fours (if you used ice cube trays, simply turn the petits fours out of the trays). Place them on a plate or lined tray, allowing a little space between them. Return the petits fours to the freezer for 2 to 3 hours. Bring the petits fours to room temperature 20 to 30 minutes before you want to serve them, and decorate with a topping of your choice. The petits fours can also be stored in an airtight container in the freezer for up to 3 months.

SPONGE CAKE WITH BLACKBERRY JAM AND THYME

Wild blackberries can grow almost anywhere. When I was younger, you could find them on abandoned pieces of land, in hedgerows, along roadsides and railtracks, etc. But they seem to be less common these days. Wasteland has been used and people's gardens are cleaned up, so there isn't much unclaimed space left for the blackberry. It's a shame, because we need these pieces of land to preserve the wild plants and the insects that live on them. Maintain your garden a little less, and you will have more time to make this delicious jam to layer into a sponge cake. The jam is made with little sweetener and thickened with chia seeds, so there is no need for lengthy boiling.

Serves 8

for the cake
½ cup plus 1 tablespoon chilled aquafaba (see page 135), whisked into stiff white peaks
1 cup whole-grain flour
2 teaspoons baking powder
½ teaspoon vanilla powder
pinch of salt
⅔ cup coconut blossom sugar
½ cup natural plant-based yogurt

for the jam
9 ounces blackberries (thawed, if frozen)
1¼ cups water or apple juice
1 tablespoon fresh lemon juice
2 to 3 tablespoons maple syrup or brown rice syrup
½ teaspoon vanilla powder
1 teaspoon fresh thyme leaves
¼ cup chia seeds

to decorate
4½ ounces blackberries
fresh thyme leaves

Preheat the oven to 350°F and line the bottoms of two 8-inch springform pans with parchment paper.

To make the cake, combine all the dry ingredients in a bowl. Using a spatula, gently fold in the yogurt and aquafaba until evenly mixed.

Divide the batter evenly between the lined cake pans. Bake for 20 to 25 minutes, until a skewer inserted into the center of each cake comes out clean. Remove the cakes from the oven and let cool in the pans for a few minutes, then turn out onto wire racks and peel away the parchment paper. Invert the right-side up and let cool.

Meanwhile, make the jam. Combine the blackberries, water or apple juice, lemon juice, maple syrup, vanilla, and thyme in a pan and bring to a gentle boil over low heat, stirring frequently to prevent it sticking. When the mixture is bubbling, cook for 3 to 4 minutes, then mash the blackberries with a fork. Remove from the heat and stir in the chia seeds. Set aside to thicken, about 10 minutes. (This can be done in advance.)

Spread half the blackberry jam over one cooled cake layer and place the other layer on top. Spread the remaining jam over the top and dot with fresh blackberries and thyme leaves.

LEMON AND BLUEBERRY POLENTA CAKE

After a 40-minute drive from my French home, following roads that get smaller and smaller, I finally arrive at a spot where, in midsummer, you can pick your own blueberries. Nowhere will you see advertisements for this spot; people just seem to know. You see them walking back to their cars laden with pounds of blueberries for the year to come. I normally pick about 8 kilos (nearly 18 pounds) of blueberries, but they never last more than a month. The blueberries are eaten straight or turned into blueberry and banana ice cream, blueberry dressing (see page 21), and this blueberry cake. Blueberries and lemon are a match made in heaven, and this polenta cake is beautifully light, thanks to the aquafaba.

Serves 6 to 8

¾ cup fine polenta

½ cup plus 2 tablespoons almond flour

¾ teaspoon baking powder

¾ teaspoon baking soda

6 tablespoons aquafaba (see page 135), chilled for at least 6 hours

scant ½ cup maple syrup

5 tablespoons natural plant-based yogurt

zest and juice of 1½ lemons

10½ ounces blueberries (or substitute blackberries or, in the winter, orange slices), plus more for serving

---

Preheat the oven to 350°F and line the bottom of a 9-inch springform pan with parchment paper.

Combine the polenta, almond flour, baking powder, and baking soda in a large bowl and set aside.

Pour the aquafaba into the bowl of a stand mixer fitted with the whisk attachment (or into a large bowl, if using a handheld mixer) and whisk until stiff white peaks form, 4 to 6 minutes.

Gently fold the maple syrup, yogurt, lemon zest, and lemon juice into the aquafaba with a spatula. Carefully fold this mixture into the dry ingredients with a spatula until just combined. Gently stir

two-thirds of the blueberries into the batter. Scrape the batter into the cake pan and gently press the remaining blueberries on top.

Bake for about 40 minutes, until a wooden skewer inserted into the center of the cake comes out clean; if not, it needs a minute or two longer in the oven. Remove the cake from the oven and let cool in the pan for a bit, then turn it out onto a wire rack to cool completely. Serve with a dollop of coconut yogurt or Cashew Sour Cream (see page 17) and extra fresh berries.

APPLE CINNAMON CAKE WITH CHAI DRIZZLE

The smell of a warm apple tart with cinnamon just instantly brings me back to my childhood at my grandparents' house. On autumn weekends my grandfather would make a tart using the apples from his allotment, which he so carefully maintained. I watched him making the cake, and although this vegan version is completely different, I know he will like it.

Serves 8 to 10

for the cake
6 tablespoons chilled aquafaba (see page 135)
scant 2 cups whole-grain spelt flour
  (or use gluten-free flour)
1½ teaspoons baking powder
1½ teaspoons baking soda
2½ teaspoons ground cinnamon
¾ cup plus 3 tablespoons coconut sugar
pinch of salt
¾ cup natural plant-based yogurt
2 medium apples, cored and coarsely grated

for the chai drizzle
5 tablespoons raw white cashew butter or white
  almond butter
¼ cup maple syrup
1 teaspoon vanilla powder
1½ teaspoons ground cinnamon
½ teaspoon freshly grated nutmeg
seeds from 1 cardamom pod
small pinch of freshly ground black pepper
1½ teaspoons grated fresh ginger
pinch of salt

Make the cake. Preheat the oven to 350°F. Line the bottom of an 8-inch springform pan with parchment paper.

Pour the aquafaba into the bowl of a stand mixer fitted with the whisk attachment (or into a large bowl, if using a handheld mixer) and whisk until stiff white peaks form, 4 to 6 minutes. Set aside.

Sift the flour into a separate bowl and add the baking powder, baking soda, cinnamon, coconut sugar, and salt. Mix until combined, then gently mix in the yogurt, whipped aquafaba, and apple.

Transfer the batter to the lined pan. Bake for 50 to 60 minutes, until a wooden skewer inserted into the center of the cake comes out clean;

if not, bake the cake for 5 minutes more, then check again for doneness.

Remove the cake from the oven and let cool for a bit in the pan, then turn it out onto a wire rack to cool completely.

Meanwhile, make the drizzle. Combine all the drizzle ingredients in a blender and blend until smooth. If the mixture seems too thick, add a little nut milk, 1 tablespoon at a time, to thin it. Be careful, though: the more liquid you add, the runnier the drizzle will become. Once the cake has cooled completely, set it over a sheet of parchment paper (still on the rack) and pour over the chai drizzle.

CINNAMON AND RAISIN BREAD WITH ALMOND MARZIPAN

Stol is a sweet Dutch bread filled with raisins that has an almond paste in the center. It is eaten at Christmastime and at Easter. Other European countries have similar breads, such as pannetone in Italy and *osterbrot* in Germany. The one thing typically Dutch is the almond paste in the middle of the *stol*. This almond paste or marzipan often contains egg, or sometimes cream: not very vegan. So I wanted to make my own version of this bread. It's a nice breakfast bread (with some nut butter) or it can be served at tea time.

Makes one 10-inch loaf (serves 10 to 12)

1 cup raisins
½ cup plus 2 tablespoons apple juice
1 teaspoon active dry yeast
3 tablespoons coconut sugar
¾ cup plant-based milk
1 tablespoon ground flaxseeds
2½ cups whole-grain spelt flour
2 teaspoons ground cinnamon

for the almond paste
¾ cup plus 2 tablespoons almond flour
5 Medjool dates, pitted
¼ cup apple juice

Put the raisins in a small bowl with the apple juice and set aside to soak.

In another small bowl, combine the yeast, coconut sugar, and 3 tablespoons of the plant milk. Stir well and set aside for about 5 minutes. The mixture may begin to fizz a bit, but if it doesn't, that's fine. This yeast mixture is a good start for your bread to leaven.

In a third bowl, combine the flaxseeds with 3 tablespoons water. Set aside for 5 minutes to thicken (this will be your flaxseed "egg").

Combine the flour, yeast, flaxseed "egg," cinnamon, and remaining plant milk in a large bowl. Start to knead the mixture. If it feels a bit too dry, add a little more plant milk or water. If it is too wet or keeps sticking to your hands, add a little flour (but not too much; often the dough will improve after a couple of minutes of kneading,

and too much flour will result in a dense bread).

Knead the dough in the bowl for a couple of minutes, then turn it out onto a lightly floured surface and knead for 8 to 10 minutes more. Transfer the dough back to the bowl and cover it with a clean towel. Set aside in a warm place to rise for 2 to 3 hours, until doubled in volume (you can also do this the night before you want to bake the bread).

Make the almond paste. Combine the almond flour, dates, and apple juice in a small blender or food processor and blend until a smooth paste forms. Roll the paste into a log shape about 10 inches long, wrap it in parchment paper or plastic wrap, and refrigerate for at least 30 minutes. The taste will improve with time, so this can be made the night before, too. When the dough has doubled in volume, drain the raisins and work them into the dough.

Form the dough into a log on a floured surface and flatten it a bit, then place the log of almond paste running lengthwise down the center of the dough. Fold the sides of the dough over the almond paste and turn over the entire loaf so the seams are underneath. Let rise for 30 minutes more.

Preheat the oven to 350°F and line a baking sheet with parchment paper. Transfer the dough to the lined baking sheet and bake for 40 to 50 minutes, until the bread looks golden brown and sounds hollow when tapped on the underside. Remove the bread from the oven and let cool before slicing and eating.

TIP:

Make this bread truly festive by choosing from the following options to make it your own: swap out the raisins for chopped apricots, sugar-free dried cranberries, or chopped dates; enhance the flavor by adding 2 teaspoons organic orange zest; add a handful of your favorite chopped nuts; or swap 1 teaspoon of the ground cinnamon for ground cardamom. To decorate, you could sift coconut flour or ground xylitol (birch sugar) over the top for a snowy finish.

GOLDEN TURMERIC MILK

This warming, aromatic, and sweet drink is colored and flavored with turmeric and other spices. Golden milk, also known as *haldi doodh* in Hindi, has its origin in Ayurveda (the Indian traditional medicine system). It is now very popular and served in healthy juice bars and cafés all over the world. I prefer to drink it at a certain friend's place, because she makes an incredibly delicious version. Her secret is to add Medjool dates and leave the milk to simmer for a long time. This recipe is inspired by her turmeric milk.

Serves 2 or 3

3 cups plant-based or nut milk of choice
1 thumb-size piece fresh ginger, peeled
  and sliced
1 thumb-size piece fresh turmeric, sliced, or
  2 teaspoons ground turmeric
1 cinnamon stick

5 cardamom pods, lightly bruised
pinch of black pepper
1 star anise pod (optional)
1 teaspoon lemon or orange zest
½ teaspoon vanilla powder
2 Medjool dates, pitted

Put all the ingredients in a pan and bring to a gentle boil over medium-low heat. Reduce the heat to low and simmer for 20 to 30 minutes. Strain the milk through a sieve into a blender.

Add the dates from the sieve, but discard the rest of the solids. Blend the mixture until frothy. Pour into mugs or glasses and serve.

TIP:
This milk can be drunk hot or cold, or mixed with chia seeds to make a golden chia pudding.

INDEX

ACKNOWLEDGMENTS

Thank you to dear Dick and Olivia for your support and the love you give me everyday. I am grateful for the warmth and love I have received from my parents, who planted the seed for my healthy food passion. I am thankful and humble for the support and guidance I get from Jos and Saskia regarding food and health. Big thanks to my sweet friends Anne, Armijn, Albert, Suzanne, Alja and Robert, who always believed in and supported my culinary work. Brecht, for making me treats when I am tired and just for being such a dear friend. Thank you Suzanne and Tamara for inspiring food get togethers and for your positivity. I'd like to thank all of my family and friends for their positivity and kindness.

Thanks to the people that bought my first book *Vegan in 7* for their support. It means the world to me knowing that so many people are cooking plant-based food and are positively contributing to their health, the health of others and our planet. I am grateful for my many followers on Instagram (@ritaserano) for the positivity and kindness I receive. Without them, there wouldn't be a book in the first place. Social media, if used wisely and independently, can be such a wonderful platform for making connections with people all around the world. Here people can contribute to each others' dreams, learnings and teachings on different levels and from different cultures. Their support inspires me every day to create delicious and healthy plant-based recipes.

Thank you to Kyle Books and the whole team for making this book come alive and making my food dreams come true. I especially would like to thank Judith Hannam, my editor Tara O'Sullivan and her assistant Sarah Kyle for making me a part of the whole book creating process. Clare Winfield for the gorgeous photography, Joss Herd and India for the beautiful food styling, Linda Berlin for getting me gorgeous props and Georgia Vaux for designing this book. Furthermore I would like to thank copy editor Stephanie Evans and the production team Nic Jones and Gemma John.

And without any doubt I would like to thank you all, who are now reading these lines. Grab my hand and use this book to be Vegan for Good!